FATHER BROWNE

A Life in Pictures

D1609655

Father Frank Browne SJ

FATHER BROWNE

A Life in Pictures

E. E. O'Donnell SJ

Wolfhound Press

First published 1994 by
WOLFHOUND PRESS Ltd
68 Mountjoy Square, Dublin 1

Father Browne prints are available from Davison and Associates,
69b Heather Road, Sandyford Industrial Estate, Dublin 18.

British Library Cataloguing in Publication Data
A catalogue record for this book is available from the British Library.
ISBN 0 86327 436 6 paperback
ISBN 0 86327 459 5 hardback

Typesetting: Wolfhound Press
Cover and text design: Jan de Fouw
Prints: Davison & Associates
Printed in Ireland by Betaprint International Ltd

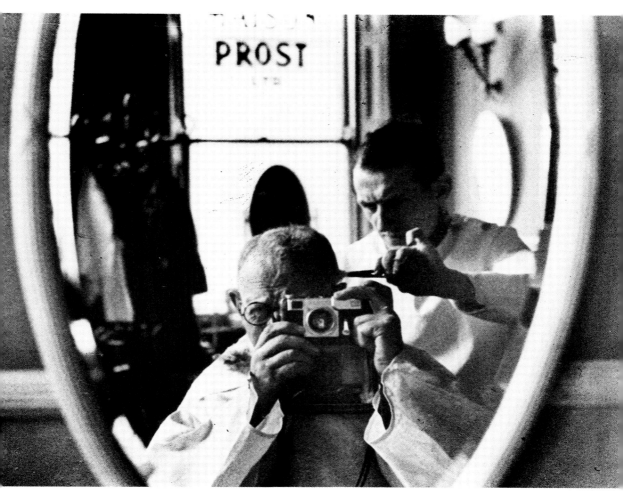

'Self at the Hairdresser's'. Taken by Father Browne at Maison Prost Ltd, Dublin, 1942

BY THE SAME AUTHOR

HISTORY

The Annals of Dublin
Wolfhound Press

PHOTOGRAPHY

Father Browne's Ireland
Wolfhound Press

The Genius of Father Browne
Wolfhound Press

Father Browne's Dublin
Wolfhound Press

Father Browne's Woodland Images
Society of Irish Foresters

RELIGION

The Sacrament of the Sick

Confession Today
Irish Messenger Publications

SOCIOLOGY

Northern Irish Stereotypes
College of Industrial Relations

CONTENTS

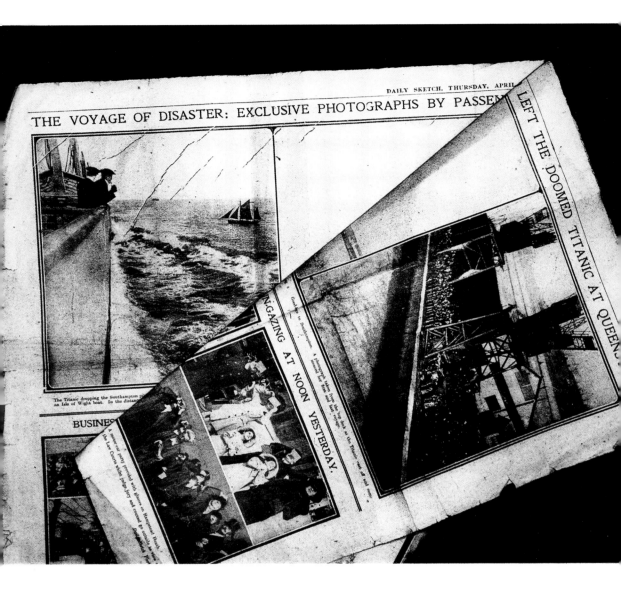

The Voyage of Disaster: Exclusive Photographs by Passengers who Left the Doomed Titanic at Queenstown.

London's Daily Sketch, *18 April 1912, with photographs by Frank Browne*

INTRODUCTION

Father Browne of the *Titanic* is how many people depict the Jesuit priest who is the subject of this biography. This, in some ways, is strange since there are only about eighty photographs of that unfortunate liner in Father Browne's Collection of 42,000 pictures. Moreover, photography was of secondary interest to a priest who had dedicated his life to the service of the Gospel. Nevertheless, it was in April 1912 that Father Browne made his name when his photographs of the maiden voyage of the *Titanic* appeared on the front pages of newspapers across the world. Although he lived for another forty-eight years after the *Titanic* disaster — eventful years as we shall see — Father Browne's name remained associated with the liner and he gave frequent public lectures on that subject.

Up to about 1950 Father Browne's name was a household one in Ireland and in photographic circles worldwide. By the time of his death in 1960, at the age of eighty, that name had begun to fade from public consciousness. Most of his contemporaries in the Jesuit Order were already dead and many of his younger confrères were unaware of his past glory. His trunk full of negatives, all neatly captioned and dated, was consigned to the Jesuit Province Archives where it lay unopened for a quarter of a century.

When I came across that trunk by accident in 1985, the negatives were deteriorating rapidly because they were mainly on nitrate-based material. It would cost a small fortune to save the Collection. The Jesuits are extremely grateful to Allied Irish Bank and to its assurance subsidiary, Ark Life, for coming to the rescue. The sponsorship of the conservation work was a generous and enlightened one. The Collection has now been transferred to safety-film and indexed. And Father Browne's name has become a household one once more.

In other words, Father Browne's story does not end with his death. His posthumous fame continues to grow. Television producers, newspaper editors and advertising agents are making increasing use of his photographs. Exhibitions of his work have been held in several countries and the list of books of his pictures is continually growing. Acclaim from the critics is mounting all the time and there is a constant demand for more information about the man behind the camera.

It is in response to such demand that I have written this book.

Frank's grandfather, James Hegarty, who was Lord Mayor of Cork (photographer unknown)

CHAPTER ONE

The Lad from Cork

Francis Mary Hegarty Browne, the youngest of eight children, was born in the Sunday's Well suburb of Cork city in the south of Ireland in 1880. He came from a well-to-do family who lived in a substantial house on Buxton Hill.

His mother, née Brigid Hegarty, was a daughter of the Lord Mayor of Cork, James Hegarty, a prominent personality in local politics for decades. A Justice of the Peace, he married Ellen Forde in 1832.

Sad to say, Brigid Browne died of puerperal fever just six days after Frank was born. Curiously, only well-off women died of that disease in those days. Surveys have shown that the poor, who could not afford doctors, rarely contracted it. This has led to the conclusion that puerperal fever was unwittingly transmitted by gynaecologists whose hygienic standards left something to be desired.

Brigid Hegarty was born at her parents' house, 'Ardfellan', on Sunday's Well Road in 1840. She married James Browne in 1866, bringing him a handsome dowry, including one of her father's tanneries on Blarney Street.

James Browne, Frank's father, was in the milling as well as the tanning business. From Charleville, County Cork, he was one of the three sons of Robert and Margaret Browne (née Mullins). His eldest brother, another Robert, was to become the Bishop of Cloyne of whom we shall hear more anon. James himself was a Justice of the Peace.

Both of Frank's parents were highly religious. His father was a Tertiary of Saint Dominic and his mother a Child of Mary, spiritual organisations well known for their charitable deeds. It is hardly surprising to learn that one of their daughters became a nun and two of their sons became priests.

Frank's eldest brother, James (born 1869), became a doctor. He emigrated to England and practised as an eye specialist at Southwark Hospital, London, where he signed the death certificate of Bram Stoker,

Frank's mother, Brigid (photograph from memorial card)

author of *Dracula*, stating the cause of death as 'venereal disease' — a choice of words that rarely appeared on such a document.

The eldest sister, Mary (born 1870), became a nun. Having spent some years in the papal household at the Vatican, she returned to Cork and taught at the Ursuline Convent, Blackrock. Her name in religion was Mother Josephine. Next came Margaret (born 1872), the only one of the girls to marry. While working as a nurse in England, she married Dr Robert Martin of Birkenhead whose surgery was in Rodney Street, Liverpool.

Robert was the next child but, sadly, he died as a baby in 1873. Ellen (born 1874) became her Uncle Robert's housekeeper. She worked at the Bishop's House, Queenstown (Cobh) throughout his long reign as Bishop of Cloyne from 1894 to 1935.

William (born 1876) became a priest. For most of his priestly life he, too, worked for his Uncle Robert. He was the Bishop's secretary for many years and then became Parish Priest of Blarney, County Cork. He died after a short illness in 1938. The seventh child was a boy, Joseph. He died when just a few months old in 1878.

Frank himself was born on 3 January 1880, and baptised in the Cathedral of St Mary, Cork.

Frank's baptismal certificate

Left: Frank's father, James; Right: Frank aged four and a half (both photos by Francis Guy)

The first extant photograph of Frank was taken at the age of four and a half when his father brought him to the studio of Francis Guy in Cork.

As a five-year-old child, presumably because of his mother's death, Frank was sent to the newly-opened Bower Convent in Athlone. Frank and his brother, William, were among the first boys to attend that school, run by the sisters of La Sainte Union, which catered for both boys and girls at that time. (It was not until 1927 that a separate school for boys was opened at Killashee, near Naas, County Kildare.) Frank spent six years at Our Lady's Bower and was very happy there. In later life he often returned to the Athlone convent school and was friendly with many of the Sisters there. In 1984, the 'Centenary Issue' of *Bower Memories* published the names of the first pupils. The 'First Register of Pupils' is reproduced opposite.

When he had completed his primary education, Frank returned to Cork in 1892 and spent one year at Christian Brothers' College, St Patrick's Place. Unfortunately, the college enrolment book where his name appears has not been completed. Indeed Frank is the only boy on the page without an address.

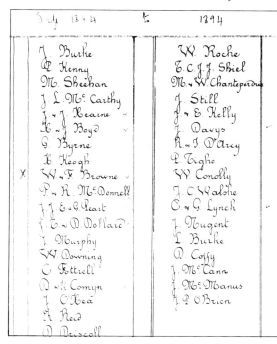

Above left: Page One of First Register of Pupils, Bower Convent, Athlone
Above right: In sailor suit, aged six (portrait by Francis Guy, 1886)
Below: Frank Browne's sisters, Ellen and Margaret, Cobh, 1950

Above: Frank Browne's birthplace at Buxton Hill, Cork (photograph by E.E. O'Donnell)
Below: The Hegartys' home on Sunday's Well Road, Cork (photograph by E.E. O'Donnell)

Above: Frank's brother, Father William Browne in hospital, 1938
Below: Christian Brothers' College, Cork, student register, 1892

At this time Frank's father was still living at Buxton Hill. He must have found the task of managing a large and young family a daunting one. Less than a year later, his sister (who lived in Ranelagh, Dublin) offered to look after Frank while he attended the Jesuit day-school, Belvedere College. That was the first of many years that Frank would spend in Belvedere: he was to return there later as a teacher and as a priest.

His aunt died at the end of 1893, so again there was a problem regarding Frank's secondary education. This time he was sent to the Vincentian Fathers at Castleknock College in County Dublin as a boarder.

Secondary education was conducted along classical lines in those days, which was fortunate for Frank because Greek and Latin were his

Aged sixteen with bike (studio portrait)

strongest subjects and he would pursue them later at University level. He was also good at English. Mathematics bored him but he studied French and Italian with success; he would appreciate this grounding in modern languages later when he lived in Italy. In neither Belvedere nor Castleknock did he study physics or chemistry: scientific subjects were simply not part of the curriculum.

Gregarious by nature, Frank took an active part in all the school field games. Thanks to his strong physique, he was an automatic choice for the first XV in rugby. Castleknock played this game with distinction at the time, as it did in later years when he returned to photograph the college team in action.

Frank Browne's secondary education was completed with a Grand Tour of Europe in 1897. Equipped with a Kodak camera for the first time, he travelled with his brother William through France, Italy, Switzerland and Germany. These first photographs, taken at the age of seventeen, already show signs of the expertise that was to follow.

Despite the relatively primitive photographic equipment of the age, and despite the slowness of shutter speeds, Frank had an intuitive grasp of composition, a talent that was to be fostered later on when he studied

'Half-time and lemons' — Rugby action at Castleknock College

St Peter's Basilica, Rome, 1897

Italian art in some depth. To help convey his talent for composing photographs with artistic line and balance, all the pictures in this book have been reproduced in their entirety. Nothing has been 'cropped'.

On leaving Italy in 1897, Frank paid the first of his several visits to Venice. From this jewel of the Adriatic he retraced his steps into Switzerland where he took many photographs around Lake Lugano before crossing the Alps into Haute Savoie. From Annecy he took the train to Paris, then returned to Ireland and joined the Jesuits.

Piazza San Marco, Venice, 1897

Belvedere Community at Moll's Gap, Carrantuohill, County Kerry, 1910

CHAPTER TWO

A Jesuit in the Making

On his return from the Continent, on 7 September 1897, Frank Browne entered the Society of Jesus at its novitiate in Tullabeg, near Tullamore in County Offaly. Formerly a boarding-school that was amalgamated with Clongowes Wood College in 1886, St Stanislaus' College was a barrack-like edifice, affectionately known as 'The Bog'.

On arrival, Frank had to surrender his camera as a 'superfluity'. For the next two years he went through the regular routine of a Jesuit novice, rising at 5.25 a.m. each day and doing an hour's meditation before breakfast — which was eaten in silence. A quarter of an hour's 'voice production' in the garden — which stood to him afterwards as a preacher — was followed by 'indoor works' which kept the house in shape. Strict discipline, in every sense of that word, made for a tidy ship. For the rest of the morning, the Master of Novices went through the Jesuit rules and constitutions. This was followed by the fifteen-minute examination of conscience that preceded dinner at one o'clock. An uplifting book was read aloud during dinner.

In the afternoons, an hour's recreation was followed by 'outdoor works' that kept the grounds in shape. Spiritual reading and a further half-hour's meditation came before supper, as the 6 p.m. meal was called. Another period of recreation followed supper, but this time the novices could speak only in Irish. At any other time of the day, incidentally, they could only converse, when necessary, in Latin. Before going to bed at 9 p.m. there was a further examination of conscience and the novices prepared their 'points' for the next morning's meditation so that these would seep in during the night.

This routine was broken only on Thursdays and Sundays. On Thursdays, in fixed companies of three, the novices went for long walks that took them all over County Offaly. Frank particularly liked to visit the monastic ruins of the county but he was not able to photograph them at this time, an omission he would make good later. On Sundays there was soccer, played with much exuberance and pent-up energy.

During their first year in the noviceship, the *Spiritual Exercises* of St Ignatius were given to the newcomers for thirty days in complete silence: a Long Retreat that was rightly considered to be the high point of the programme. As for many of his confrères, this retreat inculcated in Frank a profound and permanent love for the Mother of God. Mary, of course, had always been close to the heart of Frank Browne. Remember it was his middle name.

On 2 September 1898, the tragic news reached Tullabeg that Frank's father had drowned while ocean swimming at Crosshaven, County Cork. For years he had cycled to Crosshaven every day at dawn for his morning swim. Frank's eldest brother, James, happened to be on holiday in Ireland this September. To him fell the hard task of signing his father's death certificate.

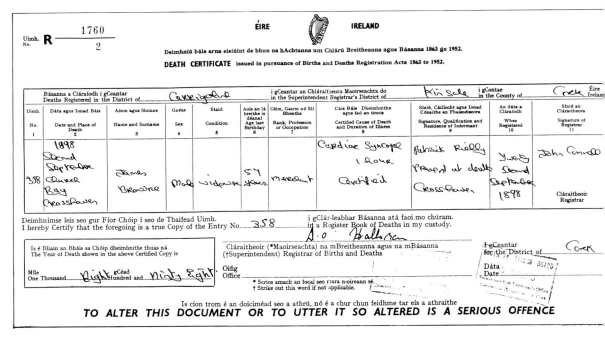

On the feast of Our Lady's Birthday, 8 September 1899, Frank took his First Vows of poverty, chastity and obedience at a moving ceremony that concluded his noviceship. He could now write the letters 'SJ' after his name, which he was proud to do for the next sixty-one years.

Next day he moved from the pollution-free fields of Offaly to the big smoke of Dublin.

For the three years beginning in the autumn of 1899, 'Mister' Frank Browne (as he was called up to his ordination to the priesthood sixteen years later) was a student of the Royal University of Ireland at St Stephen's Green, Dublin. This was the University College founded by Cardinal Newman where Fr Gerard Manley Hopkins SJ had been Professor of Greek until his death in 1889. Frank studied Greek there, as well as Latin and English. It is interesting to note that another Old Belvederian, James Joyce, was a strict contemporary for these three university years. Since Jesuit students were still not allowed to have cameras, however, we have no Browne portrait of the writer as a young man.

Joyce and Browne had much in common: both of their fathers came from Cork and both of their families originally came from Galway. The Brownes and the Joyces were numbered among the ancient tribes of that city. James and Frank had both been to school at Belvedere and both were given to philosophical speculation. Whereas James was just out of school and of an introverted disposition, Frank was twenty-two years old in 1902 and tended to be more of an extrovert. 'Mr Browne, the Jesuit' features (favourably!) in the pages of *Finnegans Wake*. Indeed the juxtaposition of the names Browne and Nolan in that book — besides alluding to the Dublin publishers of that name, to the philosopher, Bruno of Nola, etc. — might well refer to Frank Browne and a Jesuit contemporary of his, T.V. Nolan.

Joyce, too, was interested in photography and was soon to develop an interest in cinematography. He opened Dublin's first cinema, The Volta, on Mary Street, in 1909.

While attending the university classes in the building that is now known as Newman House, the 'Juniors' (as scholastics were called at this stage of their Jesuit formation) were housed in the upper storeys of the building next door. The community was a poor one and meals were said to be barely adequate. Rumours about the rats in the kitchen getting into the soup-stock have been greatly exaggerated. (Hopkins did die of typhoid, but it was of an unusual type and nobody else in his community was sick at the time.)

Although not as strict as the régime in the novitiate, the Jesuit Junior's life was still organised along fairly rigid lines. Rising at 5.55 a.m., the hour's meditation was still done before breakfast and the examination of conscience was done twice daily as in the noviceship. Then the

Juniors would attend their university lectures next door but they were not allowed to fraternise with the lay-students there. Nor were they permitted to take part in university games. Instead, they played soccer against the Jesuit 'theologians' at Milltown Park on Saturday afternoons.

While Joyce and his medical student friends were men about town, the Jesuit students devoted most of their time to their studies. This is only to be expected because University College at this time (from 1883 to 1908 to be precise) was run by the Jesuits who naturally insisted on high standards from their own men. For much of this time the Juniors stayed in Tullabeg and attended lectures there, given by accredited lecturers of the University.

Frank kept his nose to the academic grindstone and graduated with an Honours BA in Classics in 1902. He kept his final university results safely: he must have been privately proud of coming second in his class at Greek and fourth in Latin.

Right: Frank Browne, on left, with two Italian Jesuits at Chieri, 1903
Above: The Holy Shroud, Turin,1903

On the morning of 31 July that year, he must have waited anxiously for the postman who would be bringing the annual 'Status', the Provincial's document which would tell him where he was to study philosophy for the next three years. The venue turned out to be a place called Chieri in Northern Italy.

The Jesuit philosophate of Chieri stood in the hilly heart of Piedmont, about eighteen miles from Turin. There were over eighty 'philosophers' in the community, Frank being the only English speaker. A professorial staff of twelve priests gave a solid grounding in the required subjects. Besides a host of minor courses, there were two major philosophical branches to be explored each year: in the first year, logic and epistemology; in second year, cosmology and rational psychology; in third year, ethics and theodicy. All of these courses were taught in Latin.

Each Wednesday afternoon was given over to a 'Disputation' at which one of the 'philosophers' had to defend a given thesis formally against two prepared adversaries, with the rest of the community in attendance. Again, all of this was in Latin. It was lucky that Frank Browne was good at Latin, having taken that subject in his Arts degree. His Latin would also have helped him to learn Italian rapidly, especially since he had covered the basics of that language at school.

On Thursday afternoons, the students were free to explore the neighbourhood on foot. Only on feast-days were they allowed as far as Turin itself.

We know little else about Frank's years in Italy, except that during the summer holidays he was free to travel around the country where he could stay, *gratis,* in Jesuit houses provided he did not stop over for more than three nights. It was at this time that he began to study Italian painting seriously and he photographed many masterpieces on a systematic basis. Florence was his favourite city, but Venice ran it a close second. While studying art in the galleries of these cities, he paid particular attention to the compositional skill of the Old Masters — an interest that would certainly be reflected later in his own photography.

Back in Chieri, at the beginning of his third year of philosophy, Frank broke his ankle playing soccer one Sunday afternoon. That injury continued to plague him for many years and he had corrective surgery performed later in Ireland ... when he photographed his foot in plaster.

At the end of that third year at Chieri there was an extremely formidable examination, called the 'Centone'. One hundred theses

Above: Florence, 1903. Opposite: Gondolas in Venice, 1904

covering all six major courses in philosophy had to be prepared for an oral examining board of four professors. Each examiner would select one of the theses and grill the unfortunate student on it for an hour. The examination was open to the public and, although the entire proceeding was in Latin, many of the intelligentsia of Turin would attend. Frank passed with flying colours.

On his way home to Ireland in the summer of 1905, he visited the art galleries of Milan and Genoa. While in the latter city, he made sure to pay his respects at the tomb of Daniel O'Connell who died there in 1847.

Before travelling home through France, Frank Browne spent a few days at the Jesuit college in Monaco and afterwards wrote an article on the colourful history of that establishment which had been of great importance to the Order when it was expelled from France.

Then, from the tables of the Casino at Monte Carlo, he returned to the desks of Belvedere College, Dublin.

After philosophy, the next stage of a Jesuit student's formation is called 'Regency', a period spent teaching boys at secondary school. Frank was assigned to Belvedere.

The College of St Francis Xavier had been founded in Hardwicke Street in 1832 and had moved to Belvedere House on North Great George's Street in 1841. Although the school was well established by the time Frank came to teach in it, there were less than two hundred boys on the rolls and there were only twelve Jesuits on the staff. Then, as now, the college prided itself on its extra-curricular activities. Frank Browne threw himself into these with energetic abandon. During the first of his five years as a teacher, he founded *The Belvederian*, the Camera Club and the Cycling Club.

In the first issue of the college annual, Frank wrote a spirited editorial and contributed his article on Monte Carlo.

The Camera Club which (like the college annual) is still going strong taught boys the elements of photography and provided dark-room facilities. It also required its members to exhibit their photographs at a college exhibition and to attend its monthly meetings which were often addressed by guest lecturers. An annual report on the activities of the club was published in *The Belvederian*.

The college annual, for the five years that Frank was its founder editor, also published regular features on the developing art of photography.

Many of the members of the Camera Club were also in the Cycling Club, no doubt encouraged by the directorship of 'Mr Browne' — as Frank would have been called by the boys. Certainly the photographs of the Cycling Club outings that appeared in the pages of *The Belvederian* show that most of the members had cameras. Remembering the condition of the roads and of pneumatic tyres in the first decade of this century, it is surprising to see how far afield the cyclists ranged: up to Mellifont in County Louth, down to Blessington in County Wicklow and over to Clane in County Kildare.

Clane was the nearest village to the Jesuit boarding-school in County Kildare, Clongowes Wood College. Frank often visited his contemporaries who were on the teaching-staff there. On one of these visits he was brought out for a spin in a new-fangled machine called an automobile.

Besides these extra-curricular duties, Frank taught Latin, Greek and English to the senior boys of Belvedere. Second-hand accounts of his excellence as a teacher have been handed down. Suffice it to say that if he were a poor teacher he would not have retained his senior classes.

In 1909 a rather special summer holiday came Frank's way. His Uncle Robert, the Bishop of Cloyne, brought him to Rome by sea via Lisbon. It was at this time that Mary Browne was serving in the papal household. She was able to make arrangements for uncle and nephew to have breakfast with His Holiness. Afterwards, Frank was able to photograph Pope (now Saint) Pius X.

During the normal summer holidays the Belvedere community used to go on holidays to County Kerry, staying in a hotel near Killarney. Frank would bring his camera along. (The Director of the Camera Club, of course, *had* to have a camera.) He took some interesting photographs of the senior Fathers perched rather professionally on horse back.

The rest of his time in the college passed without incident and in 1911 Frank moved south of the Liffey to begin the penultimate stage of his Jesuit training at Milltown Park.

Above: Belvedere Community at Carrantuohill, County Kerry, 1910

Above left: The Tomb of Daniel O'Connell at Genoa, 1905. Above right: Frank Browne (second from left) in new car outside the castle at Clongowes Wood College, 1908
Below: The Jesuit College at Monaco, 1905

Above: European Jesuit students with radio apparatus, Milltown Park, Dublin, 1911
Below: Ordination group, 1915, with Father Browne seated beside Bishop Browne
(photograph by Lafayette)

Jesuits study theology for four years, being ordained priests after the third of these. The Irish theologate was in Milltown Park. (When the Jesuits acquired that property in 1858, the address was 'Near Dublin'; now it is a fairly central suburb.)

The routine for the 'theologians' was more or less the same as in the philosophate with daily lectures in Latin on major and minor subjects. Major subjects, spread over the four years, were on dogmatic and moral theology; the minors included Church History, Patristics and Hebrew.

In his first year at Milltown, Frank was appointed 'Beadle' of the 'theologians', their liaison-officer with the superiors and professors. This post was traditionally reserved for the most efficient member of the group.

Discipline was still strict. Dublin city, for instance, was 'out of bounds', the boundary line being the Grand Canal. Many of the students were interested in photography and a dark-room was provided for their experiments. Frank was considered to be something of an expert by his confrères and used to give classes for beginners. Other experiments involved the use of radio apparatus. The foreign scholastics were especially interested in these and used to endeavour to make contact with their native countries on the mainland of Europe. Poland, Germany and Hungary were among the countries contacted.

Frank's studies continued placidly. All was plain sailing until suddenly, on 3 April 1912, he received a letter that would change the course of his life. The letter came from the White Star Line and it contained a first-class ticket for the first two legs of the maiden voyage of the *Titanic*.

CHAPTER THREE

RMS *Titanic*

The letter he received from the White Star Line wished Frank 'an enjoyable trip' aboard its newest liner, the largest ship afloat. His ticket for the voyage was addressed to him at the Bishop's House, Queenstown, because it was Uncle Robert who had paid his fare.

Frank often visited his uncle in Queenstown (Cobh) where he developed a keen interest in transatlantic liners. He became friendly with the masters of the tenders that brought passengers, mail and baggage out to the ships at anchor in Cork harbour. Both before and after 1912, he photographed these vessels inside and out: Cunarders as well as White Star Liners, German and American ships with their passengers and crews. On shore he took pictures of the various procedures carried out before embarkation: the transfer of mails at the railway station, the bills of lading being signed, emigrants having their eyes examined for glaucoma by an American doctor before being allowed to travel to the United States.

It is likely that Frank's camera was a gift from his uncle. Bishop Browne certainly gave a present of a Kodak to his other nephew, William. The bishop encouraged the two brothers in their work and had a dark-room fitted up in his house. He was a staunch adherent of the previous Pope, Leo XIII, who in 1867 had encouraged the emerging art of photography. In his short story, 'Grace', in *Dubliners*, James Joyce has Mr Cunningham say: 'I remember reading that one of Pope Leo's poems was on the invention of the photograph — in Latin, of course.' So, as well as providing the ticket (which must have cost a pretty penny in those days), Bishop Browne probably purchased the instrument with which Frank was to record the famous voyage.

The morning of Wednesday 10 April, found Frank on the platform of Waterloo Station in London, ready to board 'the first and last *Titanic Special*'. Among those he photographed at the station was the millionaire J.J. Astor, staring rather imperiously at the young cleric with the camera.

THE NEW WHITE STAR LINER "TITANIC" (45,000 TONS) NEARING COMPLETION ;
DOCKED IN THE LARGEST GRAVING DOCK IN THE WORLD.   BELFAST, FEBRUARY 1912.

Postcard purchased aboard the Titanic

The express left London at 9.45 a.m. and an elegant breakfast was served en route to Southampton. There the train pulled up alongside the dock. Although he was expecting a big ship, Frank was astonished by the immensity of the liner. His first glimpse of the *Titanic* was from the first-class gangway which led out of an upper storey of the station. He stopped to photograph the second-class gangway 'over one hundred and fifty yards away'. Both stem and stern were out of sight.

On stepping aboard the liner, he was handed a plan of the ship in order to help him locate his stateroom, number A37. This plan still exists among his other memorabilia of the voyage. There is a note in Frank's handwriting on the top, pointing out that although the plan is headed *Titanic* this is actually a plan of the sister ship, *Olympic*. The note goes on to add that the latter ship differed from the *Titanic* in some minor respects. One difference was that the plan he was given had no staterooms numbered A36 or A37. Thomas Andrews, the Managing Director of Harland and Wolff who built the liner in Belfast, helped Frank to find his stateroom since he was looking for A36 for himself. A steward gave them the helpful advice that it was 'somewhere for'ard'.

They eventually found their quarters just at the top of the Grand

Staircase. For future reference, Frank penned in its location on his plan, showing his private entrance hallway, his sitting-room, bedroom and w.c. The luxury of the suite must have contrasted sharply with his uncarpeted cubicle in Milltown.

Next Frank went to explore the ship, purchasing a postcard of the *Titanic* nearing completion in Belfast. In their book on the liner, John Eaton and Charles Haas wrote in 1986:

> *Titanic* postcards are prized by collectors. Bargains may still be found in some shops and at some postcard shows but, typically, the price of *Titanic* postcards has risen dramatically in recent years, with few discernible links between the commonness of the cards and the prices realised.

This being the case, one wonders what collectors would pay for a postcard actually purchased on board the ship.

Before long, the rumble of the engines could be heard and most of the passengers headed for the decks to watch the departure for Cherbourg. Just after leaving its moorings, the *Titanic* very nearly collided with the *New York*, an American liner which had been tied up nearby. Frank took some dramatic pictures of the close call and described how the steel hawsers of the *New York* snapped like gunshots as she was dragged from her moorings.

It was evening when the ship reached Cherbourg where twenty-two passengers went ashore and 274 were taken on board. From the harbour a French observer reported:

Passengers having their eyes examined for glaucoma at embarkation point, Queenstown, 1912

Perhaps then, more than at any other time, she was the lovely ship that people thought her to be. Her outline was etched clearly in light, with each porthole gleaming like a star, and the mast-head lamps winking in the wavering breeze.

The *Titanic* left Cherbourg at 8.10 p.m. on the second leg of the voyage that would bring her to Queenstown. Before dinner Frank said Mass privately in his stateroom, A37.

Next morning the sun rose bright and early. Frank Browne was there to photograph the event at 6.45 a.m., captioning his picture 'The *Titanic's* first Sunrise'. Before breakfast he went and tried out some of the equipment in the gymnasium. He had a chat with the physical education officer, Mr T.W. McCawley, who gave him a signed card. His photograph of the exterior of the gymnasium appeared in Dr Robert Ballard's book on *The Discovery of the 'Titanic'* where it is contrasted with the grim picture of the rust-encrusted structure on the bed of the Atlantic Ocean.

After breakfast there was plenty of time for more photographs of different parts of the liner, passengers of three classes and members of the crew, including Captain Edward Smith walking alone along the Promenade Deck. Frank was the only person ever to take a photograph of the ship's Marconi-room. It shows Mr Harold Bride at the controls, and the caption tells us that he was 'afterwards saved'.

Another photograph shows a small boy whipping his spinning-top on the Saloon Deck, watched by his father and another passenger. Twenty-five years later, the London *Weekly Illustrated* would describe this as 'the most romantic photograph ever taken'. Let me explain why.

Early in April 1912, a rich Frenchman living near Nice decided to abscond with the family governess, taking his two sons, aged four and two, along with him. Hiring a car under an assumed name, he drove to Cherbourg, changed his name again (this time to Hoffman) and sailed on the *Titanic*. Frank Browne became friendly with the children during their first morning at sea. His photograph of the elder boy is captioned 'The Children's Playground'.

Both the father and the governess were lost in the catastrophe. The boys had been handed into one of the life-boats. They were rescued and taken to New York by the *Carpathia* and became known as 'the *Titanic* orphans'. Some weeks later, the boys' mother happened to see Frank Browne's photograph in a Spanish newspaper. Recognising her son, she travelled to New York where she was able to reclaim her children

Front page of London's Daily Sketch, *18 April 1912*
The top photograph is captioned 'The Children's Playground'

who were on the point of being adopted by Mrs Benjamin Guggenheim, the widow of one of the liner's victims.

Incidentally, when the father's body was recovered and taken to Nova Scotia for burial, the local Jewish rabbi there claimed all the coffins bearing Jewish names. So the Roman Catholic 'Mr Hoffman' was accidentally buried in the Jewish graveyard at Halifax.

Frank made numerous other friends during his short voyage and continued to correspond with survivors and with relatives of the deceased for years after the tragedy. An American family offered to pay

J. J. Astor at Waterloo Station, London, 10 April 1912

his fare for the third leg of the *Titanic's* passage to New York. From the Marconi-room, Harold Bride sent a message to the Provincial Superior of the Jesuits in Dublin asking if Frank could stay on board. When they reached Cork harbour there was an answering message for Frank. It said, succinctly, 'GET OFF THAT SHIP — PROVINCIAL'.

In later years, Frank Browne used to say that it was the only time that Holy Obedience had saved a man's life! Anyhow, off that ship he had to get. And from the tender at Queenstown he took the last extant photograph of Captain Smith — gazing, ironically, into a life-boat.

When news of the *Titanic* disaster reached Ireland, Frank was already

Above: The Browne family at Milltown Park, Dublin, for Frank's ordination, 1915
Below: Fr Willie Doyle SJ, 1914
Opposite page: Bells — two cousins of Father Browne at St Colman's Cathedral, Cobh, 1915

Father Browne as military chaplain (with his brother William
and Bishop Browne of Cloyne) before leaving for the Front, 1916

and Bar and the *Croix de Guerre*. He was also decorated by the King of
the Belgians and was described by his commanding officer, Colonel
(later Field-Marshal Earl) Alexander as 'the bravest man I ever met'.

For some interesting details of Father Browne's time as a chaplain,
we are indebted to Professor Alfred O'Rahilly's life of William Doyle
SJ, a colleague who died in the trenches. The two Jesuits served together
on the Somme, at Locre, Wytschaete and Massines Ridge, at Ypres,
Amiens and Arras. Father Browne first met up with his fellow Jesuit
early in December 1916. O'Rahilly wrote:

Father Doyle gives a humorous description: 'Picture a good, respectable,
deep Irish ditch with plenty of water and mud in the bottom; scrape a

fair-sized hole in the bank, cover the top with some sheets of iron, pile sandbags on top; and you have my dwelling. The door serves also as window and lets in not only light and air, but stray cats and rats galore and many creepy-crawly beasties, not to mention rain, snow and at times a breeze which must have been hatched at the North Pole.' It was in this dug-out that Fr. F.M. Browne S.J. met Fr. Doyle in December, 1916.

A subsequent chapter of O'Rahilly's book tells us that on 6 June 1917, at 11.50 pm when Fr Browne and Fr Doyle reached

the little sandbag chapel which they had used when holding the line. There they lay down for an hour's rest on two stretchers borrowed from the huge pile waiting nearby for the morrow's bloody work. Leaving their servant fast asleep through sheer exhaustion, the two chaplains got up at 1 a.m. and prepared the altar. Fr. Doyle said Mass first and was served by Fr. Browne, who, not having yet made his Last Vows, renewed his Vows at the Mass, as he always did at home at Corpus Christi. It was surely a weird and solemn Renovation.

This meeting took place on Wytschaete Ridge and there was, indeed, grim work to be done later that day. It was over a month later before the two men managed to get a break. Also on Wytschaete Ridge, Father Browne won his first Military Cross, accompanied by this citation:

He went forward with the battalion under very heavy fire and spent the whole day tending wounded and helping stretcher-bearers to find them under machine-gun fire. He showed splendid zeal and disregard for danger.

Above: 'The Gas and the Terror,' 1917. Overleaf: 'The Mud and the Shells,' 1917 (page 48) and 'With the Irish Guards at the Somme', 1917 (page 49).

O'Rahilly continues:

> The new Bishop of Arras, Boulogne and St. Omer, Mgr. Julien, was to make his formal entry into St. Omer on 14th July, 1917. Through the instrumentality of Fr. Browne, with the ready compliance of General Hickie, it was arranged that there should be a church parade in his honour on Sunday 15th. About 2,500 men came down. Fr. Browne said Mass and Fr. Doyle preached.

In a long letter to his brother, Father Browne described the scene:

> ... And lo! they were coming. Through all the various doors of the church they came, the 9th Dubs. marching in by the great western door, the 8th Dubs. through the beautiful southern door, the 2nd Dubs. coming into the northern aisle. Rank after rank the men poured in until the vast nave was one solid mass of khaki ... [Fr. Doyle] in his sermon spoke wonderfully of the coming of the Old Irish Brigade in their wanderings over the Low Countries. It was here that he touched daringly, but ever so cleverly, on Ireland's part in the war. Fighting for Ireland and not fighting for Ireland, or rather fighting for Ireland through another ... At the end of Mass, the Bishop in a neat little speech thanked the men for the great honour they had paid him. 'With all my heart,' said the Bishop, 'I am going to give my blessing to you, officers and men of the British Army, children of our sister nation, Catholic Ireland. May God, by a just compensation for sacrifices accepted in common, bring to an end the interior conflicts which rend the nations. And if there still remain legitimate aspirations of the Irish people to be satisfied, I bless your hopes and ask of God their realisation.'

It is noteworthy that Father Browne could recall these words verbatim. Next day it was back to the killing fields.

On 15 August 1917, the day before his comrade's death, Father Browne wrote again to his brother:

> Fr. Doyle is a marvel. You may talk of heroes and Saints, they are hardly in it! I went back the other day to see the old Dubs. as I heard they were having, we'll say, a taste of War. No one has yet been appointed to my place and Fr. Doyle has done double work. So unpleasant were the conditions that the men had to be relieved frequently. Fr. Doyle had nobody to relieve him and so he stuck to the mud and the shells, the gas and the terror.

Early in 1918, Father Browne met another Irish chaplain who was to remain a friend for life. A secular priest, Joseph Scannell also came from Cork and went on to become one of that city's most eminent priests. He became the first chaplain to the forces of the Irish Free State and later became President of St Finbarr's College, Farranferris, Parish Priest and Dean of Cork. Monsignor Scannell died in 1961.

Father Scannell frequently wrote home about the bravery and daring of his Jesuit colleague. It is in Father Browne's own handwriting,

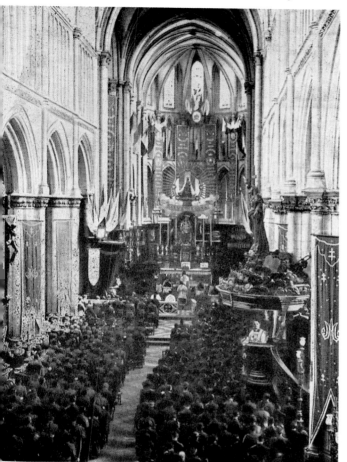

"During the Battle of Nieppe Forest in April, 1918, the Headquarters Company were shelled out of the farm at Verte Rue. They forgot to take this flag and I, seeing it, saved it from falling into the hands of the Germans. I refused to return it to the Company saying that it was *mine* by right of war — as 'they had left it behind'."

Above left: Mass in St Omer Church, 15 July 1917. (Courtesy of Longmans)
Above right: Flag of Irish Guards, with Father Browne's explanatory note, 1918,
Left: Father Browne's ration-book, Germany, 1919

LEAVE OR DUTY · RATION BOOK Serial No. S 24 N?
SOLDIER OR SAILOR.

1. Holder's Name } *Rev. J. M. Browne MC SB J*
2. Unit or Ship *A.C. attd. att. of Irish Guards*
3. Proceeding from *France*
4. Beginning of leave or duty *13/8/18*
5. End of leave or duty *26/8/18*
6. Is holder proceeding at end of leave or duty on Active Service Abroad or Service Afloat ? } *Yes*
7. Signature and Rank of Officer issuing }
8. Unit or Ship of Officer issuing *Commdg. of.*

N. 9.

Overleaf
Page 52: 'The Watch on the Rhine,' Cologne, 1919
Page 53: Rudyard Kipling (in bowler hat) with Irish Guards at Warley Barracks, Essex, 1919

however, that we can still read the note which accompanies a flag of the Irish Guards among his souvenirs of Passchendaele.

> During the Battle of Nieppe Forest in April, 1918, the Headquarters Company were shelled out of the farm at Verte Rue. They forgot to take this flag and I, seeing it, saved it from falling into the hands of the Germans. I refused to return it to the Company saying that it was *mine* by right of war — as 'they had left it behind.'

After the war had ended in November 1918, Father Browne advanced with the Irish Guards into Germany. He spent most of 1919 with them in Cologne and Bonn, taking many photographs during that year. In Wellington Barracks, London, the headquarters of the Irish Guards today, there is a magnificent album of his work entitled 'The Watch on the Rhine'. Embossed in gold letters on the morocco cover is the name, Major F.M. Browne, SJ, MC.

Another, and more homely, reminder of his year in Germany is the ration-book which he brought home. The remaining coupons suggest that he wasn't particularly partial to cheese!

Chaplains, Father Browne and Father Scannell at Arras, 1918

To my dear friend Father Browne
In memory of happy days in the Irish Guards
during World War 1. — *Alex.*

Karsch portrait sent by Lord Alexander to Father Browne

It was during 1919 that Father Browne spent some weeks with the Irish Guards at Warley Barracks in Essex. There he met Rudyard Kipling who had lost a son in the Irish Guards during the war and who was then engaged in writing a history of Father Browne's regiment. The courageous chaplain is mentioned frequently in the second volume of *The Irish Guards in the Great War.*

On 12 August 1919, while on a short home leave, the chaplain was able to attend the consecration of St Colman's Cathedral in Cobh. This marked the culmination of Robert Browne's career as Bishop of Cloyne: he had added the tallest spire in Ireland to the building which he so beautifully decorated for the previous quarter of a century.

When he retired from the army towards the end of 1919, Father Browne wrote a touching letter to his commanding office on his way home to Ireland. From the Queen Hotel, Chester, he wrote a two-page letter to Colonel McCalmont of Mount Juliet. The key sentence reads:

> I shall ever cherish the memory of my years with the Regiment and I can assure you that its interests will ever be very near my heart.

The *Irish Guards Association Journal* of February 1961 carried an obituary notice on Father Browne, in which Lord Nugent wrote:

> Everyone in the Battalion, officer or man, Catholic or Protestant, loved and respected Father Browne and he had great influence for good. He was a brave man in the true sense for he was conscious of danger but never allowed shells or bullets, which he hated as much as any of us, to divert him from his duty. Where the wounded or dying lay, there Father Browne was to be found to give them comfort and peace. ... A great Christian, a brave and lovable man, we who knew him so well will always be grateful for his friendship and for the example that he set.

Lord Alexander shared this opinion and remained a friend of Father Browne for the rest of his life.

CHAPTER FIVE

The Home Front

In 1919 Father Browne was thirty-nine years of age and had been in the Jesuit Order for twenty-two of those years. But he had still to complete his Jesuit training. The final stage of his formation, called 'Tertianship', was normally done immediately after theology. In his case it was deferred for the three years he was with the Irish Guards.

Tertianship entailed a return to the novitiate at Tullabeg for a third year (*tertio anno*) of noviceship, designed by St Ignatius Loyola as a reminder of where one had started and giving the opportunity for refurbishing one's spiritual life.

The régime was exactly as in the noviceship, including the indoor and outdoor works, the silence, the day punctuated by the sound of bells summoning the tertians to their next task. Above all, it included another Long Retreat of thirty days. The *Spiritual Exercises* always meant a lot more to tertians than they did to novices.

It is not hard to imagine that this year must have been a difficult one for Father Browne, coming so soon after his shattering years with the army. Moreover, his lungs were giving him trouble as a result of the mustard-gassing in 1918 and his hearing was already beginning to give cause for concern, probably because of artillery-fire. Eventually he would have to use a hearing-aid.

One difference between tertianship and noviceship was that he was allowed to keep his camera: a major concession as far as Father Browne was concerned. Before leaving Germany in 1919 he had acquired a new camera, a Plaubel 'Makina', which took excellent pictures and he was very pleased with the results. He wrote to his brother about it:

Dearest Will,

I enclose a few prints of St. Ursula's taken with my new camera. It was bright when I started work but was almost dark by the time I'd finished. I almost gave up in despair. I can say that I'm surprised by the results. Tell me what you think. By the way, I'm going to ask you to repay me later.

A short time later he wrote again:

> Dearest Will,
>
> I am sending you two photos taken with the new camera. The photos of the kiddies I took this morning because I was anxious to get some photos of some kiddies here with their sledges. 2nd because I wanted to get a proof for you of the value of the f4.5. It was almost too dark: I was afraid of a complete failure and even tried to alter the speed from 1/25 to 1/10 after I had set the shutter. This cannot be done without having first released the shutter, so I chanced it. f4.5; time 1/25. It is quite well exposed and the only fault is my bad judging of distance. I am no good at that. I *never* was.

With the help of a new Zeiss 'Universal' range-finder, this was a problem that Father Browne was soon to solve. He spent most of Thursdays and Sundays in Tullabeg practising for perfection with the camera, just as he spent the rest of the week perfecting his spiritual life.

Up to 1920 hardly any of the Browne photographs were taken indoors. Now he began to experiment and achieved quite satisfactory results with home-made floodlights.

In July 1920, he completed his tertianship and was assigned to teach in Belvedere College once more. He resumed the editorship of *The Belvederian* and took over the running of the Camera Club and the Cycling Club once more.

During his first term in Belvedere, on 31 October, he cycled up to the Vice-regal Lodge in the Phoenix Park to make a personal appeal to Lord French on behalf of the Irish patriot, Kevin Barry. To no avail: the Belvederian boy was executed in Mountjoy Jail next morning.

No record remains of Father Browne's stance during the Anglo-Irish War or the Civil War. Among the few photographs taken during these troubled years was a series showing his native Cork after it had been destroyed by the 'Black and Tans' (British auxiliary security forces) in December 1920.

On the feast of Candlemas, the festival of the Blessed Virgin Mary on 2 February 1921, Father Browne took his Final Vows as a Jesuit. These included the fourth vow of special obedience to the Pope taken by 'honours' Jesuits. He was now fully fledged.

In 1922 he was appointed Superior of St Francis Xavier's Church, on Gardiner Street, Dublin. The saying among Jesuits at the time was that it was 'more important to be a Gardiner Street Father than a rural Rector' — so his new appointment must have been a major promotion.

The Belvedere community was very sorry to lose him and one of the

Tertians at Tullabeg, 1920

Cork city after destruction by the 'Black and Tans', 1920

Above left: The new Superior of Gardiner Street Church, Dublin, 1922 (photo by C. Walsh)
Right: St Francis Xavier's Church, Gardiner Street, in Father Browne's day
Below: The new loudspeaker system at Gardiner Street Church installed by Father Browne

past pupils wrote in the school annual as follows:

> Belvedere sustained a very great loss this year by the promotion of Fr. F.M. Browne to the superiorship of St. Francis Xavier's, Gardiner Street. Father Browne was a man of manifold activities. He founded, during his stay at Belvedere, the Cycling Club, the Camera Club, the Touring Club, and was Editor of *The Belvederian*. In fact he took such a leading part in the social life of the College that to many of the boys Father Browne *was* Belvedere. There is another point in connection with Father Browne's work that should be emphasised, and that is the interest, the practical interest, he took in the Past Students. He was a never-failing friend to any boy who required a nomination for Guinness's or any of the Irish Banks. Belvedere is not the same without him. His interest in the Old School was shown time and again during the past year and we are very grateful to him for it. His congratulations when we won the Senior Cup were highly appreciated and his presence on the evening when we were celebrating the victory was most welcome. Everyone who knows him wishes him great success in his new field of activity.

Gardiner Street Church, designed by Bartholomew Esmonde SJ with help from the architect, John Keane, was opened in 1832 and gloried in the soubriquet, 'The Farm Street of Dublin'. (Farm Street is the location of a fine Jesuit Church in London.)

As Superior, Father Browne was responsible for assigning the other members of the Jesuit community to their various duties in the pastoral apostolate. Although it was not a parish church at the time, it was a very busy place, running many specialised sodalities and providing a pulpit for the numerous famous preachers of those days. Dubliners flocked to Gardiner Street for the Novena of Grace, the Sacred Heart Devotions and for the lectures of Professors from Milltown Park.

Father Browne carried out many practical improvements, such as the installation of a loudspeaker system and the replacement of antiquated central heating.

In the middle of all this activity, his health began to deteriorate. His lungs were increasingly giving him trouble. His doctor recommended dry air and a warmer climate, so early in 1924 he left to spend two years in Australia.

Top: 'The Rip' off Melbourne
Right: Crewman exercising
on the Arundel Castle, (both
photographs taken in 1924)

CHAPTER SIX

Australia and Elsewhere

Father Browne sailed for Australia on 12 March 1924, leaving Falmouth on board the liner *Port of Melbourne*. For the first week of the voyage, the sea was calm but his health was poor. He was thankful for the attention of the ship's doctor.

As the weather warmed he began to feel better and enjoyed the remainder of the trip to Cape Town. He stopped over for some weeks there and took photographs all around the Cape Province of South Africa.

While he was in Cape Town he stayed with Fr John Morris who afterwards became the well-known editor of *The Southern Cross*. His photographs show a cross-section of the population ranging from children of all races playing together on the beach at Camps Bay to sophisticated adults admiring Watts' famous sculpture of 'Physical Energy' at Groote Schuur. Table Mountain, of course, dominates most of his panoramic views.

Continuing his journey to Australia on the *Arundel Castle*, Father Browne took dozens of pictures during the voyage, mostly showing the passengers at play and the members of the crew at work. When the ship arrived at Melbourne, Father Browne felt very much at home because he was met by a group of Irish Jesuits, several of whom had joined the Order on the same day as himself. Originally, Australia was a 'Mission' of the Irish Province of the Society of Jesus, so (apart from some 'natives') most Jesuits there were Irish. Today, Australia is a Province of the Order in its own right.

In Melbourne, Father Browne stayed at Werribee College which was a diocesan seminary staffed by Jesuits. It had opened its doors just one year earlier, Albert Power SJ being its first Rector. In Sydney, whose harbour he photographed before the bridge was built, he stayed at Riverview College which overlooked the harbour and also spent some time at the College of St Aloysius.

Above: Adderley Street, Cape Town, 1924
Below: Zulu foreman, Cape Town, 1924

Canvas Home at Molong, New South Wales, 1925

By this stage the photographer's health was improving. In over a thousand pictures of Australia which he took before the end of 1925, we see that he was able to attend horse-races at Melbourne, yacht-races at Sydney, cricket test matches against England at Adelaide and Brisbane, as well as sheep-shearing competitions at Kangaroobie. Furthermore, he travelled for over three thousand miles in the outback. A random selection of his photographs gives the flavour of his two years in the southern continent.

Above: Brisbane, Queensland, 1925
Below: Grand Hotel, Parkes, New South Wales, 1925

Above: Sandgate Beach, Queensland, 1925
Below: 'Me and the Elephant', Kandy, Ceylon, 1925

The return journey to England began with a voyage on the *Orama* from Perth to Ceylon, now Sri Lanka, via the Cocos Islands. In Colombo he visited Kegalle School, run by the Irish Sisters of Mercy. At Kandy he photographed the Temple of the Sacred Tooth and made an interesting portrait entitled 'Self in Rickshaw'. He also had his photograph taken beside an elephant.

From Ceylon he travelled via Somaliland and Yemen to Aden. Then, past Ethiopia, Sudan and Saudi Arabia, his ship sailed on through the Red Sea to Suez. Passing through that canal, he photographed life in Egypt on both the African and Asian banks before arriving in Port Said.

From Port Said he sailed across the Mediterranean Sea, first to Salonika in Greece and then, past Mount Etna on Sicily, to Naples. A three-day stopover there gave him the opportunity to visit Pompeii and

Opposite page: Street Scene, Port Said, Egypt, 1925
Below: Atrium of Sallust, Pompeii, Italy, 1925

El Espacho de Carbon, Algeçiras, Spain, 1925

photograph its extraordinary remains.

His next ship took him to Toulon in the south of France with its Napoleonic forts guarding the harbour; then to Gibraltar where again he stayed for three days. He took some fine pictures of the Rock itself and then crossed into Spain to visit Algeçiras and La Linea.

From Gibraltar he voyaged to Lisbon, which brought back memories of his 1909 visit, and from the Portuguese capital it was non-stop to Plymouth with a rough passage through the Bay of Biscay. After a short stay in England, Father Browne returned to his post at Gardiner Street in full health once more.

CHAPTER SEVEN

Sermons and Salons

From the end of 1925 to the end of 1928 Frank Browne was back in charge of St Francis Xavier's Church in Dublin. With his lungs cured, permanently as it turned out, his fame as a preacher increased: people would come from distant parts to hear his sermons.

His pastoral duties were central to his life but there is no need to do more than state that fact here.

It was also in 1925 that he began to photograph Dublin city extensively. In due course he would take nearly five thousand pictures of the capital, the final roll of film being shot in 1957. There are nearly 42,000 negatives in his Collection altogether, 36,000 (approximately) taken in Ireland. By December of 1925 he had taken less than four thousand photographs, a quarter of these in Australia. In other words, the bulk of his photographic work was still to come.

He continued to invite professors of theology from Milltown Park to explain the truths of Christianity in the Gardiner Street pulpit. Fr John Gannon came regularly and drew vast crowds, of which the Collection provides visual documentary evidence.

Another adventure: he took lessons as a pilot in 1926. His Dublin photographs include many of the city and suburbs taken from the air. For the most part, the quality of these was poor — as he was the first to admit — but there are several excellent views of the city and of the Malahide area in north County Dublin.

During 1926, a Doctor and Mrs Burke invited Father Browne to accompany them and their son on a motoring tour of Ireland for the summer holidays. This trip brought the Browne camera to focus on such historical and archaeological sites as Newgrange, Glendalough, the Rock of Cashel, Gougane Barra, Monasterboice and the Aran Islands. (He would visit these islands again later to photograph the life of the inhabitants in more detail.)

Later that summer Father Browne travelled to England where he had

Above: Jubilee Procession, Gardiner Street, Dublin, 1925
Below: Queues for lecture of Fr John Gannon SJ, Gardiner Street, Dublin, 1926

been asked to give a retreat to the nuns of the Bar Convent, York. As well as attending to the Spiritual Welfare of the sisters, he took dozens of photographs of that ancient city, its walls and gates, its shambles and its Minster.

Before returning to Ireland, he visited the Jesuit boarding-school, Stonyhurst College, in Lancashire. He recalled that Conan Doyle had been a pupil there and had used Stonyhurst and its grounds as the setting for his masterpiece, *The Hound of the Baskervilles*. (The first-year class in Stonyhurst — as in Belvedere and Clongowes Wood — was called 'Elements'; hence the word, 'Elementary', when Sherlock Holmes is speaking to Dr Watson.)

By 1927 Father Browne was a member of the Photographic Society of Ireland and of the Dublin Camera Club. Peter Walsh, Curator of the Guinness Hop Store exhibition centre in Dublin, takes up the story:

> On 16 June 1927, a fellow member of the Camera Club, William Harding, gathered a little group of 'doubting friends' (including Frank Browne) together in an upstairs room in Jury's [Hotel, Dame Street, Dublin]. Harding infused them with a large dose of his own infectious enthusiasm and perseverance, and within a few weeks — with Harding as Director — the first ever Irish Salon of Photography was created and it went on to become the outstanding success of Dublin Civic Week 1927. Father Browne's Jesuit colleague, Fr Paddy Kennedy SJ from Belvedere, an ornithologist of some repute and later author of *An Irish Sanctuary*, judged the Nature Section of the Salon. Father Browne, along with General O'Duffy and Mr Justice Hanna, was one of the vice-presidents under the presidency of Sir John Lavery.

Exhibits at the Salon included work from England, France, Germany, Austria and Australia as well as from the United States of America.

These Salons continued to be held in Dublin every two years until World War II broke out in 1939. Father Browne remained a vice-president throughout this period. He also exhibited some of his own work and won numerous prizes. His first recorded prize — of a guinea, which was the top award in the competition — was for a photograph captioned, 'The Census Paper', taken in 1927 at Cheeverstown, County Dublin.

William Harding died in 1928. In the catalogue for the following year's Salon, Father Browne himself contributed a foreword by way of appreciation:

> To the work of the Irish Salon of Photography in 1929 no Foreword cold be more fitting than an Afterword on the genius of him to whom the Salon owes its inception.

Top left: Father Browne with a Bristol Fighter, Baldonnell Aerodrome, County Dublin, 1926
Right: On tour with the Burkes at Monasterboice, County Louth, 1926
Below: Prize-winning photograph, 'The Census Paper', Cheeverstown, County Dublin, 1927

On June 28th last, death claimed William Harding, friend, photographer and idealist; but in the work he set amoving still lives the spirit of his enthusiasm. It was in those days of troubled peace following the World War that he first came into our lives. When other minds were set on the stern realities of political change his could vision only a fellowship of art, in which all lovers of the camera would unite. It mattered not to him whether they were young or old — nay, truly, it mattered much to him that they should be both old and young — for in the vision he unfolded, the schoolboy with his 'Brownie' stood beside the veteran artist whose name had grown familiar to generations of photographers.

As Michael Angelo saw his 'David' in the block of blackened marble that for centuries had lain in Florence, beside Giotto's tower, William Harding saw, in the immature attempts of boyhood, possibilities of an Irish School of Photographic Art, worthy to rank beside those of England, France or Germany. What mattered it to Harding that others doubted! Knight errant at heart, he would enter the lists alone to win consideration for his Lady of the Light, Photography. Who of the members of the Dublin Camera Club can ever forget the eagerness with which he sought — and found — for almost every meeting a new venue, when, one after another, the older ones were closed to us? Who does not recall his enthusiasm for *The Camera*, that forum of Literary Art, to which his persuasive personality attracted from every continent, writers and workers in the Science and Art of Photography?

In its pages he retold to the photographic world his vision, till men began to wonder could it be realised. Dublin's first Civic Week brought him, in 1927, the long sought opportunity. Gathering about him a little group of doubting friends — I will remember the first informal lunch hour meeting in an upstairs room of a Dublin hotel — he infused into them some of his own enthusiasm and persevering, in spite of official indifference or half-hearted approval, he made the First Irish Salon of Photography the outstanding success of Civic Week.

It was, surely, a well-deserved triumph for this Dreamer of dreams that Ministers of State and Civic functionaries and more than thirteen thousand citizens should throng the house of his dreams come true. In it they saw the finished works of German, French and English Masters of the Camera: in it, too, they saw the work of Irish schoolboys, not merely admitted on sufferance, but even judged worthy of award. Harding's wish had ever been that in his dream-house Irish workers should hold the place of honour, to prove that even in this land of hazy distances and chequered sunlight artists could be found to catch the elusive softness of her light. But Irishmen misunderstood his aim, and many, far too many, of their exhibits were brought from foreign shores.

That Irishmen should overlook the beauty of their motherland was a sad surprise to William Harding, the Irishman. Nothing daunted, he would win them yet. With this object in view he chose as the jewel of this year's Salon, the portraiture of Ireland in all her moods — let the artist be who he may. Thus would he turn the eyes of Irish photographers to their own Ireland:

The West Front of York Minster, 1926

thus would he lure from sunnier lands artists whose skill could truly portray the softness of her countryside and the everchanging charm of her skies.

Has his aim been realised? Friend, with you lies the answer, and, as you pause to give it, forget not to bless the memory of him whose legacy to you and Ireland is a greater realisation of Ireland's beauty in Irish Camera Craft.

I have quoted this piece in full because I believe it gives us some insight into the way Father Browne himself thought about photography. It helps to explain why he gave so much commitment to

Irish Salon of Photography, 1927

President: SIR JOHN LAVERY, R.A.

Vice-Presidents:

THE HON. MR. JUSTICE HANNA, K.C.   REV. FRANCIS C. BROWNE, S.J.   GENERAL O'DUFFY
(Commissioner, Garda Siochana)

Judges:

THOMAS BODKIN, ESQ., B.L.   ALFRED WERNER, ESQ., F.R.P.S.   REV. P. G. KENNEDY, S.J.
(Director, National Gallery of Ireland)   (Belvedere College). *Nature Section*

Executive Committee.

Director of Salon: WILLIAM HARDING, F.C. (Editor of THE CAMERA)

W. N. ALLEN   MRS. J. C. LOUGHRIDGE   P. L. PEWRIS   JOHN ROWLAND
(Past President, P.S.I.)   (Past President, P.S.I.)

HENRY M. DOCKRELL   MISS L. LONG   MAJOR R. H. PLEWS   T. H. SCANLON, B.L.
(President, Dublin Camera   (Secretary, Civics Institute   (President, Photographic
Club)   of Ireland)   Society of Ireland)

H. de B. JONES   THOMAS H. MASON   GEORGE PRESCOTT   GEORGE J. SINGLETON
(Past President, P.S.I.)   (Vice President, Dublin
Camera Club)

ALFRED WERNER, F.R.P.S. (Past President, P.S.I.)

Hanging Committee: MESSRS. T. MASON, J. ROWLAND and T. H. SCANLON

Hon. Organising Secretary: MRS. MAUD WALSH, U.D.C.

Foreword by the President

The photographer should bear in mind that his work can stand alone, and at its best is independent of the painter or the draughtsman. He has the means of revealing mysteries of light and air unknown to either of them, and would add more to our knowledge of the study of Nature than he would by the study of the greatest work of art that man has created.

It is my opinion that photography should be true to itself rather than an imitation of other means of pictorial expression such as wash drawing, engraving, etching, or other hand work.

JOHN LAVERY.

The following beautiful verses, written in 1867 by Cardinal Pecci (afterwards Pope Leo XIII.), express the highest ideal of camera art to-day, even after sixty years of progress :--

> Sun-wrought with the magic of the skies
> The image fair before me lies,
> Deep vaulted brain and sparkling eyes
>   And lips fine chiselling.
>
> O miracle of human thought !
> O art with newest marvels fraught !
> *Apelles, Nature's rival, wrought
>   No fairer imaging !

*(Apelles was the most famous of Grecian painters)

3

From a Salon Catalogue, 1927

what at the time some would have considered to be a pretty frivolous and esoteric pastime.

Being a Corkman, and one who often returned to his native county, it comes as no surprise to learn that Father Browne exhibited his work at the Cork Camera Club's annual exhibition. He won prizes there too, an early example being 'Georgian Splendour', which won him a medal in 1928.

All this time Father Browne's reputation as a preacher in Gardiner Street continued to grow: so much so, that his next assignment was to the Mission and Retreat Staff of the Irish Jesuits, a post he would occupy for the next thirty years.

'Georgian Splendour', Curraghmore House, County Waterford, 1928

CHAPTER EIGHT

Home Missions

The Jesuits had opened Clongowes Wood College in County Kildare as a boarding-school in May 1814. (Its name is familiar to many from the opening chapters of *A Portrait of the Artist as a Young Man*.)

The Jesuits had purchased the property from the Wogan-Browne family. Previously called 'Castle Browne', perhaps after a distant ancestor, Clongowes was one of the old fortresses which guarded 'The Pale'. Thus it stood, literally and symbolically, on the fringes of civilisation: a bastion to keep the 'Wild Irish' at bay.

When Father Browne went to stay there in 1928, the College was thriving. An impressive series of portraits of distinguished past pupils filled the length of what the boys called the 'Rogue's Gallery'. The school community was a tightly-knit unit, so the new 'Missioner' must have felt something of an outsider.

'Missioner' was the name given to members of the Mission and Retreat Staff. This was the group of eleven or twelve Irish Jesuits whose work was to give parish missions throughout the four Home Countries and to give enclosed retreats to priests, nuns, working-men and schoolchildren. Members of the team usually worked in pairs: the entire group rarely gathered together to discuss progress or methodology. Each member of the team based his teaching loosely on the *Spiritual Exercises* of St Ignatius: in this sense Jesuit missions differed from others. But there was no such thing as a Jesuit style of preaching. Any stereotype one might have in this regard is pure myth. Styles differed as much as the Missioners themselves, from the low-key and devout to the pulpit-thumping stentor. Father Browne by all accounts shunned the fire and brimstone approach. He believed in drawing the attention of his listeners on the love of God rather than terrifying them with the fear of the Lord.

When he arrived in Clongowes Wood towards the end of 1928, he knew he would not be there for long. Negotiations were already under way for the purchase of Lord Portarlington's house in County Laois which was to be used as a new novitiate and as a base where a group of the Missioners could feel at home. Meanwhile, the team was scattered among all the Jesuit houses, Father Browne being the only one with a room in the castle at Clongowes.

During 1929 he began the routine that he was to follow for so many years, travelling continually from parish to parish, mainly by train. He seems to have started his apostolate by concentrating on his native province of Munster, indeed on his native county of Cork. He gave numerous parish missions in both city and county and directed several retreats for the Sisters of different congregations, including one in his own sister's Ursuline Convent, Blackrock, in the suburbs of Cork.

The work suited Father Browne admirably. He soon found that nearly all of his work was to be done in the evenings which left him free for most of the day to pursue photography. When he was giving a parish mission in Buttevant, for example, he would find plenty of time during daylight hours to photograph the antiquities of the neighbourhood such as the old 'clapper' bridge (now demolished) which had been built by monks in the Middle Ages. If he wanted to photograph something a little further afield, the local parish priest or one of his curates might be able to take him by car. In this instance he was driven from Buttevant to Mallow to photograph the interior of its massive and well-furnished castle.

In the middle of 1930 the move to Emo finally took place. Emo Court was designed by James Gandon for George Dawson, first Earl of Portarlington, in 1790. Variously called Dawson Court and Emo Park, the Jesuits changed its name to St Mary's. After somewhat barbaric alterations had been made to the main building, the novices were brought over from Tullabeg and installed there. A curved corridor, named the Serpentine, led to a separate building to the left of the main house known (for some obscure reason dating back to the Portarlington days) as the 'Bachelors' Quarters'. It was in this block that Father Browne acquired the room that would be his haven and his photo-laboratory until 1957.

From time to time over the years, quite a few of the Mission Staff were based in Emo. Between missions they had time to compare notes and to develop a more consistent geographical spread for their labours. Among the priests who worked with Father Browne on this nomadic

'Castle Browne', Clongowes Wood College, County Kildare, 1929

apostolate were Fathers Paul O'Flanagan, Michael Garahy, William Hogan, William Stephenson, Leonard Sheil, Robert Louis Stevenson, and Launcelot Croasdaile who came from nearby Rosenallis.

Now that he had a permanent base, Father Browne was able to set up his photographic equipment more satisfactorily. He coaxed the electricians who were re-wiring the main house at Emo to do a major job on his room, giving him two batches of electric sockets, ample power-points for his growing number of accessories. He had special blinds and curtains fitted to his window so that it could be converted into a dark-room within seconds.

It was at the beginning of 1931 that he acquired a new camera, this time a 'Special Sibyl' manufactured by Newman and Guardia. Early in the following year, knowing that it would be put to good use, his Uncle Robert gave him a present of a Kodak 16mm cine-camera.

1932 was the year of Ireland's Eucharistic Congress, a Roman Catholic festival that would bring crowds of visitors, prelates and laypeople, from overseas. It would also bring together the biggest crowds of Irish people since the Monster Meetings of Daniel O'Connell in the previous century. Father Browne was present, with both still and

'Shooters Shot', Buttevant, County Cork, 1930

movie cameras, at all the main events of the Congress. He photographed the Papal Legate, Cardinal Lauri, arriving at Dun Laoghaire; Cardinal Glennon of St Louis preaching at Gardiner Street; Orthodox Church dignitaries at the grave of Matt Talbot; Ireland's oldest prelate, Robert Browne of Cloyne, attending a civic function; G.K. Chesterton attending open-air Mass in the Phoenix Park, Dublin; John Count McCormack singing the *Panis Angelicus* before over a million people; Dublin city and suburbs decorated for the occasion.

From a vantage-point on the roof of Kennedy and McSharry's on Westmoreland Street, he was able to capture in still and moving images the impressive scene as O'Connell Street began to fill with people arriving *en masse* for the final benediction of the Congress which was given on O'Connell Bridge on Sunday 26 June. His captions for a sequence of photographs are given to the minute: at 4.39 p.m. O'Connell Street is empty; at 5.00 p.m. it is beginning to fill up; at 5.30 p.m. it is full.

After the celebrations had come to a conclusion, Father Browne returned to Emo and developed his films. (For years the rest of the community would be complaining about lack of access to the bathroom

CHAPTER NINE

English Commissions

Between 1933 and the outbreak of World War II in 1939 Father Browne spent a good proportion of his life on our neighbouring island. His work as a missioner brought him to many parishes in Wales and Scotland — including the islands of Jura and Islay — but it was in England that he found himself most frequently. Nearly every year during this period he attended the annual pilgrimage at Walsingham, which was the subject of his first English movie.

While on pilgrimage to Walsingham, Father Browne used to stay with Lady Ashburnham who not only commissioned him to photograph the Shrine of Our Lady but also put her chauffeur, Boxall, at the priest's disposal. Thanks to this kind gesture, Father Browne was able to photograph many English villages that were not on any railway line, progressing from Little Snoring to Great Snoring, from Sandringham to Caister-on-Sea. At Walsingham, and also during the annual pilgrimage at Dunwich in Suffolk, Father Browne was able to record many famous preachers addressing the assembled crowds: Cardinal Bourne, Fathers Vernon Johnston SJ, Fabian Dix OP, Ronald Knox and Martin D'Arcy SJ are names that come to mind.

During the summer of 1933 Father Browne paid a visit to the Kodak Works at Harrow, near London, where he was able to photograph cameras being manufactured and where he had an important interview with the Managing Director, George Davison. Davison had been a prominent artistic photographer and a founder of a secessionist movement called The Linked Ring, in 1892. This group founded the London Salon of Photography, and it is interesting to note that Father Browne was instrumental in the foundation of the Irish Salon, with similar aims to those of 'The Ring'. 'The Ring' eventually recombined with the Royal Photographic Society in 1910. Clearly Father Browne had found a kindred spirit in photography and presumably in consequence of this George Davison arranged for him to receive a free

Above: Father Browne making motion-picture at Walsingham, Norfolk, 1933 (Photograph taken by Claude Fisher of Norwich)
Below: Lady Ashburnham's chauffeur, Boxall, having his name taken by police following an accident at Norwich, 1933

Fr Ronald Knox preaching at Walsingham, Norfolk, 1933
Below: The body of Bishop Robert Browne who died in Cobh, 1935

supply of film for life. By way of return, Father Browne used to make regular contributions to *The Kodak Magazine*. Many of these features were on the Cathedrals of England, nearly all of which came under Father Browne's photographic scrutiny during these years.

In March 1935, Father Browne had to return to Ireland urgently when he received the sad news that his Uncle Robert lay dying in Cobh. He arrived in time to photograph the Bishop's last outing in his bath-chair and took some final pictures of his favourite uncle reading his breviary beside the fire. Next day the bishop was dead. Knowing the value he had placed upon photography, his nephew continued to take pictures, showing the various groups and individuals who came to Bishop's House to pay their last respects. On the following day Father Browne photographed the funeral at St Colman's Cathedral and the burial of his uncle in a place of honour in the new cemetery close by. Then he returned to England to give yet another parish mission in Liverpool.

In England, Father Browne photographed most of the Church of

Ely Cathedral, 1934

England cathedrals and also took pictures of many of the Roman Catholic ones, some of which were still in the course of construction. He visited London on many occasions and took remarkable photographs of the capital, including several on the Underground railway system. When staying overnight in London, often he availed of Lord Alexander's standing offer of accommodation. Curiously, there is no record of his ever staying with the Jesuits at Farm Street.

It was while he was in London that Father Browne visited the British Museum which commissioned him to photograph certain antiquities of England. He gave a lot of time to this important work and afterwards, when he had returned to Ireland, continued a lengthy correspondence with the Museum. He worked directly for Mr Thomas Kendrick who went on to become a well-known Director of the British Museum.

This brings us to 1937, a year in which Father Browne was still contributing to *The Kodak Magazine*. His literary style is exemplified in what he wrote about Norwich Cathedral in April of that year:

> Norman arches, Gothic vaulting, cathedral grandeur and monastic charm, all combine to make of Norwich Cathedral a paradise for historians and photographers.
>
> Nowhere else, perhaps, in England are such varied factors united so perfectly and harmoniously within the compass of a single building. That the builders of Norwich Cathedral succeeded so eminently is a unique tribute to their skill and artistic sense. Those of us, therefore, whose ambition it is to catch with our cameras the spirit and workmanship of vanished generations are well advised to spend as long as possible close to Herbert of Losinga's beautiful cathedral. We may appropriately begin our visit at that old Norman doorway of the North Transept from the niche above which the century-old statue of Herbert looks placidly down on passing generations. He died in 1119.
>
> Coming round to the west end we can — if we are so minded — table a lively discussion as to the good (or bad?) taste of Bishop Alnwick's fifteenth century perpendicular window and doorway. There they are, facing the criticism of

all comers as they stand in aggressive contrast to the quieter and more dignified Norman work of the north and south portions of the facade. Still worse are those rows of intruding motors, parked with anachronistic vandalism right in the foreground of the only possible picture!

To get a general view of the exterior is very difficult, because on every side except the east, Norwich Cathedral is closely surrounded by buildings. Those beautiful gates — Ethelbert to the south and Erpingham to the north, with the curtain wall between them — seem scarcely able to keep the old frame houses of Tombland from invading the quiet of the Close.

Inside, we have the solid majesty of the Norman nave crowned by the most striking Gothic vault in England. The wonder of its details and the full story of its 400 carved bosses has but recently been revealed to modern eyes by the genius of Mr. C. P. Cave, who spent many months in making of it a photographic survey. It was in 1463, about 20 years after Bishop Alnwick's work on the west front, that a great fire brought the old wooden roof crashing down upon the Norman nave. Bishop Lyhart, whose quaint 'rebus' — a hart lying in water — is to be seen on many of the bosses, immediately set about the restoration, for which to-day we are so grateful.

South of the Cathedral we come to the beautiful cloister which is at once the largest surviving Monastic Cloister in England, and also the last complete survival of the Benedictine monastery beside which Herbert of Losinga began to build.

From cathedrals the photographer moved on to smaller churches. During 1937 and 1938 the Governing Body of the Church of England commissioned him to photograph the churches of East Anglia, inside and outside, concentrating on any unusual details. Herr Hitler was rattling his Luftwaffe and rumours of war filled the air. As a precaution against bomb damage, the Church of England wanted to ensure that its buildings could be restored with precision. Amateur photographers all over England took hundreds of thousands of pictures as part of this far-sighted survey. The north of Essex and all of Suffolk and Norfolk came into Father Browne's ambit.

Hardly any Church of England building in Norfolk or Suffolk escaped the photographer's lens. Indeed a whole book could be filled on this subject alone. The variety of church furnishings he chose to photograph is astonishing: from bench ends to baptismal fonts, from misericords to memorial tablets.

His notes on the Church of England churches that he photographed were extensive. On the Ranworth screen-printing, for instance:

St. Michael conquering Satan with a flaming sword — from the famous screen at Ranworth on the Norfolk Broads. This has been called 'the most

Above left: Roman Catholic Cathedral, Liverpool, during construction, 1935. Right: West Front, Norwich Cathedral, 1937. Taken on Kodak 'Verichrome' film; f8, 1/50 sec., overcast afternoon
Below left: 'Angels as Corbels', Knapton Church, Norfolk, 1938
Below right: Duke of Westminster's shooting-lodge at Plas Eglysyk, Wales, 1938

Above: Tower Bridge, London, 1936. Below left: Medieval painting of St Michael, Ranworth Church, Norfolk, 1938. Right: Saxon carving in cemetery wall, North Pickenham, 1936 (Reproduced courtesy of the British Museum)

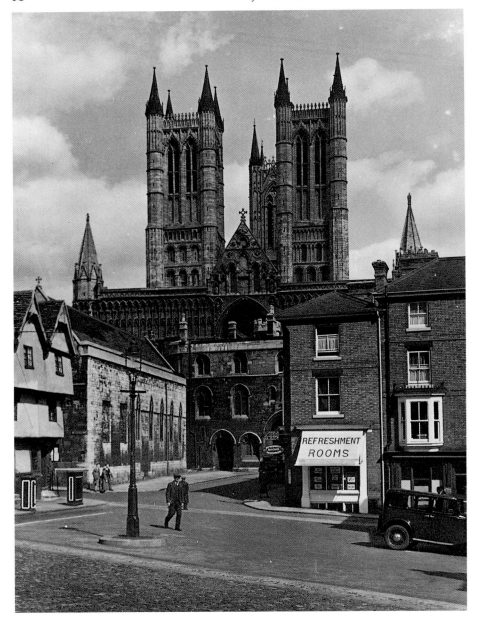

Lincoln Cathedral, 1934

cavalier St. Michael in all the records of the Middle Ages!' The Puritans damaged the painting in 1640.

Father Browne's work for the Church of England was a nice ecumenical gesture carried out in gaps between his ongoing parish missions. When we look at his English photographs as a whole and ask ourselves why he took so many of them, the answer is fourfold:

believing in 'art for art's sake', he took many pictures simply for their sheer beauty; knowing the value of local history, he knew his work would be of value to such historians in due course; he wanted to demonstrate that England was Christian as well as 'merrie'; he wished to fulfil the many and varied commissions that came his way. This work will be further detailed in the forthcoming *Father Browne's England*.

Towards the end of 1938 it was time for a break and on his way home to Ireland he was a guest at the Duke of Westminster's hunting-lodge at Plas Eglwysyk in North Wales. By the time he reached Dublin, Father Browne was feeling unwell. Appendicitis was diagnosed and he was committed to the care of the Irish Sisters of Charity at St Vincent's Hospital, at that time located on St Stephen's Green. Before his appendectomy, the photographer mounted his camera on a tripod in the operating-theatre and set it on time-hold so as to be able to caption a picture, 'Self under Anaesthetic'.

Father Browne recovered quickly and was soon on his feet again. However, 1938 was to end with another family bereavement: his brother William, Parish Priest of Blarney in County Cork, died after a short illness. Once again the Browne camera was present *post mortem*.

The personal sadness of the end of 1938 gave way to the universal horror of 1939. The world was at war once more.

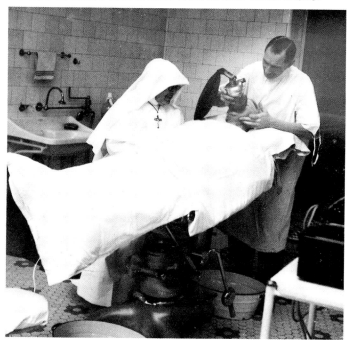

'Self under Anaesthetic', St Vincent's Hospital, Dublin, 1938

CHAPTER TEN

'The Emergency'

The years 1939 to 1945 in the Republic of Ireland were euphemistically called 'The Emergency', the republic being neutral during World War II. What Father Browne thought of de Valera's policy of neutrality remains unrecorded, as do his views on the partition of Ireland and the Civil War that followed. He simply captioned his many pictures of customs-posts on the Irish border as 'Our Divided Island'.

When the war broke out in 1939 the former military chaplain and hero of the Great War was fifty-nine years of age. Nonetheless, he was quick to volunteer his services. First he wrote to Fr Tom Vesey, the Senior Chaplain to the Forces at Wellington Barracks in London, asking what his response would be if his Jesuit superior allowed him to rejoin the Irish Guards.

Fr Vesey replied at once, saying 'we really wish you could come and join us again.' Father Browne was overjoyed and wrote straight to the Provincial in Dublin stating, more or less, that he had been invited to serve as a chaplain once more.

The Provincial, Fr Laurence Kieran SJ, soon dampened Father Browne's ardour. He replied as follows:

My dear Father Browne,

In reply to your letter just to hand, it would be best to reply [to Fr. Tom Vesey] that in the present circumstances you cannot act as chaplain.

I have had no official request for chaplains up to the present and, if and when one does come, the request will have to be carefully considered in view of the fact that this country is neutral and that there are, properly speaking, no Irish regiments now.

With every good wish,

Very sincerely in Christ,

L.J. Kieran S.J.

This disappointing news had to be passed on to Fr Vesey who replied from the Regimental Headquarters:

Emergency rations, Jesuit refectory, Gardiner Street, Dublin, 1943

Dear Father Browne,

Ever so many thanks for your letter and for its kind words. I thoroughly understand the things you say. I quite understand how you are situated but am only so very sorry that we shall not see you in the Irish Guards once more.

I deeply appreciate your effort.

Most sincerely,

Tom Vesey

During the Emergency, therefore, Father Browne had to stay at home. Travel across the Irish Sea was restricted by the activities of German U-boats so his missionary activity was confined to Ireland. He continued to give missions and retreats throughout this period, including parish missions north of the border in places like Dungiven, Armagh and Martinstown, County Antrim. He photographed several railway-stations in Northern Ireland where the name-boards had been removed in case they would be of help to German paratroops.

On the Great Northern Railway he took a picture of the notice which advised people what to do if the train was caught in an air-raid. On the Great Southern Railway he recorded the absence of sugar in the dining-car as one of the minor deprivations of the day.

Most of his travelling during these years had to be done by train: few

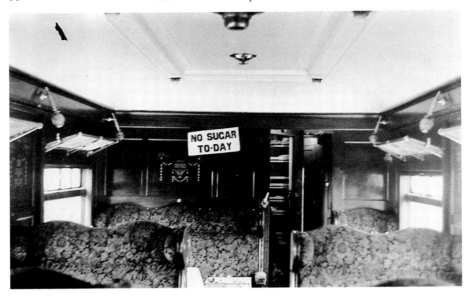

Dining-car notice, Great Southern Railway, 1941

cars were on the road due to the shortage of petrol. There was an absence of coal as well, so the trains burned turf — and ran behind schedule as a result. Millions of tons of turf, for the trains and for industrial and domestic consumption, were carried to Dublin where they were stacked along both sides of the main road in the Phoenix Park.

As the Emergency wore on, food-rationing had to be introduced: a reminder for Father Browne of his year in Germany in 1919. In Emo itself, where the Jesuits ran their own home farm, the rationing of food had little impact. The Order's Dublin houses, naturally, were as badly hit as anyone else. In St Francis Xavier's, Gardiner Street, where Father Browne used to stay whenever he was in the capital, the daily rations in the refectory were carefully laid out on a sideboard.

Father Browne continued his photographic work during the Emergency years. Still working with nitrate film, he made many nature studies in the grounds of St Mary's, Emo. For example, he spent many hours studying the life-cycle of a swan: from empty nest, to nest with eggs, to chick hatching, to cygnet being fed by pen and eventually taking to the water at Emo Lake. It is reported that the photographer spent three days lying on his stomach in the undergrowth waiting for an egg to hatch.

Another subject which absorbed him was the roosting posture of the

Left: Cygnet hatching at Emo, County Laois, 1944
Below: Kitten at Emo, County Laois, 1945

tree-creeper. The giant Californian redwood trees at Emo, called Wellingtonias, had a spongy outer bark that provided an ideal roosting-site for these small birds. Interestingly, the tree-creepers only roosted on the north-eastern sides of the trees, away from the prevailing wind. Father Browne pointed out this phenomenon to his colleague, Fr P.G. Kennedy SJ, who wrote an article on it for *The British Journal of Ornithology*. Browne photographs illustrated the text.

Other nature studies include 'Trees', 'Seasons', 'Clouds', 'Flowers' and 'Animals', with dozens of photographs under each of these headings. This last pack of negatives contains pictures of horses, donkeys, cows, pigs, goats, dogs and cats. Most of these nature photographs were taken with the new camera, a Contax 'Number Two' which Father Browne had been given by his brother-in-law in 1937.

It was about this time, incidentally, that his ankle gave way again, necessitating an operation in St Vincent's Hospital, Dublin.

An insurance policy covering the photographic equipment which Father Browne was using at this time reveals that he possessed the following:

1. Cine Kodak Camera, Model B.B. with F/1.9 Lens.
2. Kodak 76 mm. F/4.5 Telephoto Lens No. 8847 for Cine Kodak B.B.
3. Solid leather case for same.
4. Lancaster Vertical Enlarger with Watson Holostigmat Lens, Series 1.
5. Leitz Valoy Enlarger with 'Varob' Lens, 40" Column and Leitz adjustable masking-board belonging thereto.
6. Kodak Tank Developing Outfit.
7. Zeiss Developing Tank.
8. Zeiss Ikon 16 mm. Cine Projector.
9. Two Inch Lens for same.
10. Fibre Carrying-case for same.
11. Celfix Crystal Glass Beaded Cine Screen.

12. Canvas and Leather Carrying-case for same.

13. Newman and Guardia new Special Sibyl Camera with a Ross xpres' F/4.5 Lens.

14. Three Filters.

15. Zeiss 'Sonnar' F/4 Lens.

16. Leather Case for above.

17. Albada Finder.

18. Contax 'No. 2' Camera with Ever-Ready Case and 'Sonnar' F/2 Lens.

19. Zeiss 'Tessar' Wide-angle 2.8 cm. F/8 Lens.

20. Wide-angle Finder for above.

21. Tabular Four' draw tripod with turntable head in Leather Case.

22. 1 Zeiss Copying Head.

23. 2 Zeiss 'Proxar' Copying Lenses: (a) 'Delta' 2 x 42; (b) 'delta' 3.5 x 42.

24. Focusing Adaptor.

25. Focusing Magnifier.

26. Zeiss 'Universal' Finder.

Tree-creeper roosting at Emo, County Laois, 1944

27. Weston 'Master' Exposure Meter, Model 735.

28. Forster Flash Gun Reflector.

29. Ross 'Definex' Lens.

30. Linhof Press Tripod.

31. Chronograph Automatic Switch for Enlarger.

Photographers will also be intrigued to learn that Father Browne manufactured his own 'portable dark-room' in which he could change films in the open air.

Also during the Emergency, Father Browne continued to experiment with colour photography. We know that he had worked with 'DufayColor' in the middle of the 1930s but no example of this work remains in his Collection. His early colour photographs, however, still exist and have been purchased at specialist auctions as late as the 1980s. Presumably because of the expense involved in colour photography, and presumably because his standing allocation of film from Kodak did not include colour stock, he restricted his experiments to

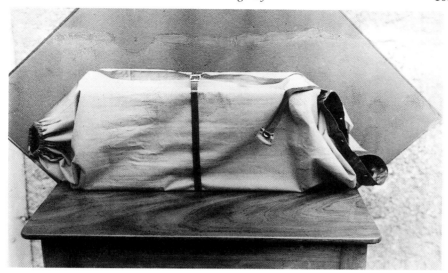

Father Browne's home-made 'portable dark-room', 1945

marketable subjects which could be turned into postcards, such as views of Croagh Patrick and of Achill Island.

Although his services as a chaplain were not required at this time, Father Browne kept in touch with the Irish Army whose ranks were considerably increased during the Emergency. In the Western Command, especially, he visited the barracks in Athlone and Galway and photographed the many diocesan colleges which stood ready to be turned into hospitals in case of the outbreak of hostilities. St Eunan's in Letterkenny, County Donegal, and St Flannan's in Ennis, County Clare, are two cases in point.

He had many relations in the Southern Command of the army and, whenever he was in Cork, he made sure to photograph them in uniform. In the Eastern Command he had friends — both officers and other ranks — in McKee Barracks and in Collins' Barracks, Dublin. The Emergency years often found him with his camera at the Curragh, County Kildare, where he enjoyed photographing the troop movements and army manoeuvres.

Finally, we should note that Father Browne's interest in the army was not confined to ground forces. He often visited the Air Corps at Gormanstown in County Meath and at Baldonnell aerodrome near Dublin where he had flown a Bristol Fighter back in the 1920s. His interest in aircraft would continue when peace-time returned.

The German forces in Italy capitulated to Field-Marshal Alexander

Above: 'Troop Movements' on The Curragh, County Kildare, 1945
Below: Letter to Father Browne from Field-Marshal Alexander, 1945

on 29 April 1945. Father Browne sent a letter of congratulations. Earlier he had sent his friend 'Alex' (who was a Northern Irish Protestant) a medal bearing the image of the Mother of God. In those pre-ecumenical days he would have had to explain that Roman Catholics do not *adore* Mary: they venerate her and ask for her intercession with her Son. The Field-Marshal took the point. He sent Father Browne a letter of thanks and told him that he would be pleased to wear the medal. When the war was over, Father Browne photographed that letter and placed it among his treasures.

And now my dear father thank you so much again for the holy medal — . I am very much touched by it and very happy to have and wear it.

your old friend.

Alex

CHAPTER ELEVEN

Semi-professional

The inaugural passenger flight between Dublin and Bristol had been conducted by Irish Sea Airways in 1936. Dublin Airport had yet to be built, so the flight left from Baldonnell. Desmond FitzGerald — whom Father Browne had taught at Belvedere — was the architect of Dublin's new airport at Collinstown in 1940. As a guest of Aer Lingus, the photographer went there to inspect progress in 1946. He kept a pass, signed by Mr E. Rooney, allowing him to take pictures in the hangars and on the tarmac. This enabled him to take photographs such as his close-ups of the 'Dakota' engines being serviced.

Later in 1946 he travelled down to County Clare to photograph the larger transatlantic aircraft at Rineanna (now Shannon) Airport. The Pan American 'Clipper' and the Trans World Airways 'Constellation' were shown disembarking their passengers outside the tiny terminal building. Once again Father Browne was able to take close-ups of the fitters in action, of the refuelling team at work, of the passengers checking-in. The pictures he took of air traffic controllers, complete with binoculars and chalk-board in the Control Tower are of continuing interest to aerophiles everywhere.

Father Browne never flew to America but he did fly to England on numerous occasions: his 'missionary' work there was in demand again after the war. He gave nuns' retreats in Beaconsfield (Sisters of the Cross and Passion), Ealing (French Sisters of Charity) and York (Sisters of Mercy), to mention but three. He gave parish missions in places like Dumfries (Scotland), Porthmadog (Wales), Northampton and Lewes (Sussex).

It was not until the early 1950s, when he had used the last of his supply of nitrate rolls, that he began to make consistent use of Kodak Safety Film. (Over three-quarters of his Collection — i.e. some 30,000 photographs — is therefore on the older unstable stock). It was also in the early 1950s that he acquired his last camera, a compact Leica. Before

Above: Collinstown Airport, Dublin, 1946
Below: Aircraft at Rineanna (now Shannon) Airport, 1946

Pilgrims at 'The Station', Glencolumbkille, County Donegal, 1950

he died, Father Browne gave his Contax to John Moore SJ and taught him how to use it for to his botanical studies. This Jesuit went on to become Lecturer in Botany at University College Dublin before moving to Lusaka, Zambia, where he is now a missionary priest. During a visit to Ireland in the summer of 1993, Father Moore kindly donated this Zeiss Contax camera to the Collection.

During the 1950s, Father Browne, who was now in his seventies, was still giving parish missions throughout Ireland. His photographs show, for example, crowds leaving these missions at Longford Cathedral, Whitehall Church, Dublin, Armagh Cathedral, Ballylongford Church, County Kerry, and St Brendan's Cathedral, Killarney. Interior shots show the 'Candle-light Closing' of missions at Portlaoise, Limerick, Galway, Wexford and Derryvolgie Avenue, Belfast.

All over Ireland there are Jesuit Mission Crosses, erected mainly in the nineteenth century, commemorating parish missions given in places like Clonmany, County Donegal and Ennis, County Clare. Father Browne photographed many of these just as he did the medieval and Celtic Crosses that dot the country. He compiled an album of 'positives' of these, entitled 'The Crosses of Ireland'. Normally, he made very few prints of his negatives, presumably for financial reasons. But he did leave nine albums of photographs, each containing about a hundred prints, in his famous trunk. Other albums are called 'People I have Met in Various Lands', 'The Cistercian Abbeys of Ireland' (two volumes), other 'Monasteries of Ireland' and 'The Cathedrals of England'.

Before moving on to more secular themes, it is worth pointing out that Father Browne photographed the many pilgrimages that take place annually in different parts of Ireland. The ones that spring to mind are at Lough Derg, County Donegal, Ardee, County Louth, Tubbercurry, County Sligo, Clonenagh, County Laois, Scattery Island, County Clare, Mount Brandon, County Kerry and Faughart, County Louth. The Irish pilgrims form an engrossing contrast when juxtaposed with their English counterparts at Dunwich and Walsingham.

During the early 1950s, Father Browne found time to become a more active member of the Irish Photographic Society. But this time he attended meetings more as a tutor than as a learner. There are photographs of him lecturing on indoor photography. 'No Divorce' was an expression he used in this regard, meaning that if one were photographing the interior and exterior of a building, then the number of arc-lamps employed indoors should depend on the amount of daylight outside. On a sunny day, therefore, one would need to use a lot more lamps than on a cloudy day: there should be no disparity between the pictures taken because the camera's

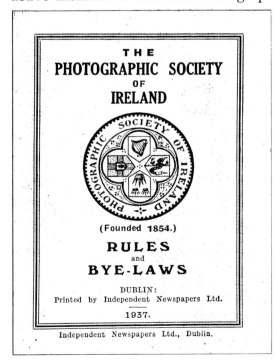

Father Browne's membership card of the Irish Photographic Society, 1950

Billiards Room, Fota House, County Cork, 1950

shutter position would remain unaltered.

He also went on many field expeditions with the Irish Photographic Society and was assigned to adjudicate amateur photographic competitions on its behalf. O'Donnell's Stockbrokers of St Andrew Street, Dublin, was just one company to use his services in this regard.

By way of practising what he was preaching about the photography of buildings, Father Browne made a point of touring the country and recording on film the Great Houses of Ireland and their owners.

The houses he photographed are far too numerous to list here. A few names will indicate the scope of this section of his Collection: Fota House, County Cork, Glin Castle, County Limerick, Rockingham House, County Roscommon, Dunsany Castle, County Meath, Birr Castle, County Offaly and Powerscourt House, County Wicklow. In Dublin the list includes the Casino at Marino, the castles at Howth and Malahide, Mespil House (which is now demolished) and Rathfarnham Castle (now a National Monument). In the Phoenix Park he photographed both Áras an Uachtaráin (the Presidential Residence) and the US Ambassador's residence in great detail.

During this period, too, various state and semi-state bodies commissioned Father Browne to work on their behalf. In 1951 the Department of Health under its Minister, Dr Noel Browne (no relation) prepared a booklet on the Mother and Child Scheme, illustrated with Browne photographs.

In 1952, the Office of Public Works, under its secretary, Mr J.W. Nolan, had Father Browne visit the Royal Hospital at Kilmainham in Dublin to photograph the antiquities and curiosities stored there before that building's restoration. The National Museum also invited him to photograph antiquities such as the Tara Brooch, the Cross of Cong and the Ardagh Chalice.

In 1953 Father Browne paid his final visit to London where he was the guest, as usual, of Lord Alexander who was then Minister for Defence in the British Government. Back in Ireland, in 1954, the Electricity Supply Board was the subject of the photographer's scrutiny. Not far from his home base at Emo, he showed the new peat-burning power-station in Portarlington during the course of construction as well as in production.

Father Browne had always been fascinated by electricity. Indeed a whole book could be devoted to his 'Irish Lights'. He photographed the first hydro-electric scheme being built at Ardnacrusha on the Shannon during the 1920s and went on to record the other such schemes at Poulaphuca on the Liffey and at Ballyshannon on the River Erne. The rural electrification of Ireland was the source of inspiration for many

Below left: Department of Health 'Mother and Child Scheme' booklet 1951 with note by Father Browne on the cover, and right his photo from page 5 of the booklet

ESB power station, Portarlington, in the course of construction, 1954

of his photographs: 'The Shadow of Progress' was how he captioned a picture showing the reflection of a new ESB pole against a whitewashed cottage in Keadue, County Roscommon.

Other semi-state bodies to utilise his services were the Irish Sugar Company — whose factories, beet-fields and beet-trains he photographed — and Bord na Móna (the Turf Board) whose pioneering activities he recorded at Lullymore, Clonsast and elsewhere in the midlands.

The Irish Travel Association (now Bord Fáilte) often published Father Browne's photographs in its tourist magazine, *Irish Travel*, and later when it started publishing *Ireland of the Welcomes*. An ITA brochure for Berehaven, County Cork, had a Father Browne picture on its front cover: on his file copy the photographer noted: 'The yachts were painted in!'

Travel and all forms of transport were subjects dear to Father Browne's heart — including, of course, aircraft and ships. As a youth and as a young man he had taken the tenders from Queenstown (Cobh) to photograph the transatlantic liners; he recorded all the ships on which he had travelled himself, including the liners to and from Australia as well as the Mail Boat between Dún Laoghaire and Holyhead and the B&I ferry between Dublin and Liverpool; he photographed yacht-races in Cork Harbour, Sydney Harbour and

Dublin Bay; in fact he snapped anything that floated, from the powerful tug at the Albert Dock in London to the humble barge on the Grand Canal in Dublin, not forgetting the trawlers at Clogherhead, Killybegs and Balbriggan.

Next we come to trains, another Browne passion. His Collection contains well over a thousand photographs of trains, taken not only in the Home Countries but in Australia, Egypt, Italy and France. His pictures of Irish trains are alphabetised neatly and show not only locomotives and rolling-stock but also the railwaymen at work. He has vivid pictures of several railway accidents and among his masterpieces are some shots he took on the 'TPO' because the Department of Posts and Telegraphs allowed him to photograph the sorters at work in the Travelling Post Office on the Dublin-Cork railway. He exhibited his picture of 'The Grasp', showing the dangling mail-bag being whipped by the passing train into the safety of the sorters' waiting net.

Father Browne lived to see the advent of the diesel-train in Ireland. Like most railway lovers, he must have lamented the passing of the steam age. Nevertheless he enjoyed at least two journeys when he was allowed to handle the controls of the new-fangled locomotives.

As regards road transport, the Browne Collection has pictures of everything from trams to donkey-tandems, from bicycles to articulated lorries, from horses-and-carts to traction engines. As one works chronologically through the photographs, the horse-drawn phaetons and landaus give way to the earliest 'Tin Lizzies' and the beautiful early Benz. Father Browne himself seems to have had frequent access to an elderly Riley motor-car: it often appears in his captions as 'Miss Riley'.

In this connection a letter received recently from Thomas Eustace of Dublin throws an amusing light on the motorist-photographer:

Dear Father O'Donnell,

I had the pleasure of presenting your book, *The Annals of Dublin,* to my father on his 78th birthday the other day. He said that he knew Father Browne well as he often went on cycling trips with him while my father was a student in Belvedere. My father's father was a busy G.P. who lived on Parnell Square [Dublin]. He had two cars, a Buick and a small Citroën and from time to time Father Browne would borrow the Buick for one of his various expeditions. One Sunday afternoon, my grandfather was trundling up the Phoenix Park in the little Citroën when the Buick roared past nearly sweeping him off the road. That apparently ended Father Browne's borrowings of the Buick!

Where was he off to at such a pace, one wonders. Was he rushing to take photographs of a 'high society' wedding (something he was commissioned to do more and more frequently during those years)? Was he off to deliver a 'Children's Holy Half-Hour' (a new devotion of his own invention)? Maybe he was going to give a 'Novena of Grace' in honour of St Francis Xavier?

Father Browne preached at this novena every year while he was on the Mission Staff. In the middle of the 1950s his services were requested by the Parish Priest of Beechwood Avenue Church in Dublin. He concluded his sermon there one evening by saying: 'Now if there are any young men, or even any not-so-young men, listening to me tonight who feel they could replace me in the Jesuit Order (because I haven't much longer to live), let them come in and have a word with me afterwards in the sacristy.'

One 'not-so-young man' — a thirty-two-year-old — was listening and did go to the sacristy to speak with Father Browne after the ceremony. Paddy Doyle joined the Jesuits and later became the Provincial Superior of the Order in Ireland.

Such was the influence of Father Browne in the pulpit. But he was correct in thinking that his preaching days were nearly finished.

Trawlers at Balbriggan, County Dublin, from the GNR train, 1956

CHAPTER TWELVE

Last Post

In 1957, after being based in Emo for the best part of thirty years, Father Browne was transferred to Milltown Park in Dublin where he had been ordained a priest forty-two years earlier. Technically, he still belonged to the Mission Staff. Old soldiers never retire. Increasing infirmity, however, curtailed his movements and he did most of his work in Dublin. He was beginning to show his years, as can be seen in a photograph taken by a friend (Graham Urch) in Brown's pharmacy on St Stephen's Green in Dublin.

During the last three years of his life, Father Browne contributed to many newspapers and magazines in Ireland and England. Most of the Dublin newspapers published his photographs, as did *The Cork Examiner*. Magazines that carried Browne features include *Country Life, The Tatler and Sketch, The Irish Digest, The Capuchin Annual, The London Weekly Illustrated, The Far East* and *Ireland of the Welcomes*.

Many individuals and organisations continued to contact Father Browne in his declining years, commissioning photographs of people and places. The Irish Countrywomen's Association, the Kildare Archaeological Society, the National University of Ireland and the Irish National Teachers' Organisation were four of the last to do so. In the library of University College Dublin at Belfield there are two magnificent albums of his late work, one commemorating a Jubilee of the INTO, the other depicting the Georgian architecture of Newman House, St Stephen's Green, Dublin.

Over the years, he sent all his photographic earnings to the Provincial Treasurer of the Jesuits, keeping a meticulous tally of the amount he had forwarded. At his own suggestion, these funds went to the formation of what he delightfully called 'Brownie Burses' for the education of Jesuit students. All told, he sent over a thousand pounds to these burses between 1937 and 1959 — a lot of money in those days.

During 1958 and 1959 Father Browne put the finishing touches to the catalogue of his Collection. Before computers, this was quite a task. He listed separately the different countries where he had worked and then made sub-sections for Archaeological Remains, Abbeys, Castles, Colleges, Convents and so on.

The most important part of his catalogue is the alphabetical list of the people he had photographed during his sixty years behind the camera. The vast majority were ordinary men and women, including ordinary Jesuits, though the list also includes some prominent names: politicians such as William Cosgrave, Eamon de Valera and Tim Healy; prelates such as Cardinals Bourne, Logue and McRory; ambassadors such as Marchese Giovanni Sali of Italy and Mgr Paschal Robinson of the Vatican; writers such as G.K. Chesterton, Rudyard Kipling and Sir Shane Leslie; members of titled families such as Lords Bective, Castlerosse, Dunsany and Rosse.

During 1959 Father Browne's health deteriorated and he was hospitalised in St Vincent's twice. He also had to spend some time convalescing at Linden Nursing Home, Stillorgan. His hearing continued to worsen and he had to use a hearing-aid. This was a large contraption which he carried prominently on his chest. He used to fidget constantly with its controls, which disrupted one of his last retreats, given to a community of nuns in Dublin. One afternoon he was hearing Confessions in the convent parlour, while several of the Sisters waited on the corridors outside. Father Browne was seated in an armchair behind a grill, fidgeting with his hearing-aid while one of the younger nuns knelt on the prie-dieu on the opposite side of the grille. Suddenly, to the consternation of those in the corridor, the young nun rushed out of the parlour in a panic. When she had recovered sufficiently, she gasped: 'He was trying to take my photograph!'

The priest's last photographs were taken, in fact, in the vicinity of Milltown Park where he focused on the neighbouring Jesuit establishments: Gonzaga College and the Catholic Workers College (now the National College of Industrial Relations). His very last pictures were of the grounds of Milltown Park itself, taken in colour.

In the summer of 1960 Father Browne was told that he was dying. Faithful to the last, Lord Alexander travelled from England to visit him on his death-bed.

The photographer photographed by Graham Urch, Dublin, 1957

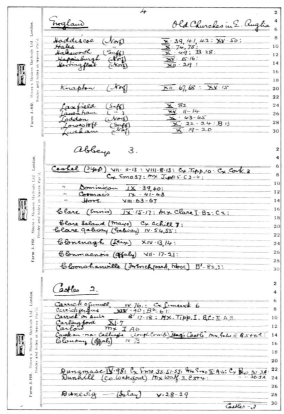

Top: Milltown Park, Dublin, 1959. The original of this photograph is in colour.
Below: Sample pages from Father Browne's catalogue, 1958

Jesuit funeral at Glasnevin Cemetery, Dublin,
where the photographer-priest was buried in 1960

He died, much lamented, on 7 July 1960. Among the many obituary notices, *The Province News* had a paragraph that can be quoted by way of summation:

> Father Browne was a most priestly man. This priestliness he carried into the pulpit. He was never cheap or frivolous. His preaching was always impressive, his words well chosen, his examples apt. He had a very friendly and sympathetic approach to his congregation. His confessional was always crowded and never hurried. There was the kindly word for everyone. With the secular clergy he was extremely popular, yet always reserved and dignified. It is the truth that he never forgot that he was a priest and a Jesuit.

Father Browne's funeral took place on 9 July 1960. Given that he took nearly 42,000 photographs during his life, it is no surprise that one of these was of the Jesuit burial-plot in Glasnevin Cemetery, Dublin, where he now rests in peace.

CHAPTER THIRTEEN

Posthumous Fame

In the Jesuit grave at Glasnevin Cemetery in Dublin lie the remains of Father Browne and of Gerard Manley Hopkins, among others. One might think the English convert to Catholicism and the Irish 'born Catholic' had little in common. Hopkins was a poor preacher with bad health who tended towards introversion and depression; Browne was the opposite, on all four counts. However, they shared a similar philosophy of life, a love of Nature in all its manifestations, a shared appreciation of the after-life, an unquenchable faith, a devotion to the Mother of God and a pride in being members of 'Christ's Company'. Both men achieved recognition early in life: Hopkins was 'The Star of Balliol', the Oxford College; Browne photographed the *Titanic*. By the time they died, however, each man's name was known to just a small circle of friends who recognised his artistic legacy. Hopkins might have died in a blaze of glory had he lived longer; Browne could have died famous had he died earlier.

Gerard Manley Hopkins is now 'the most read and the best-loved poet of the nineteenth century,' according to his recent biographer, Robert B. Martin. The Poet Laureate, Robert Bridges, preserved Hopkins' poems and published them thirty years after the poet's death. Decades later he became recognised as the father of modern poetry.

When Father Browne died in 1960, most of his contemporaries were already dead. His Jesuit confrères in Milltown Park — including his Rector — were much younger men. He had taken only a few hundred photographs since his arrival in Dublin in 1957. His brethren would have known about the *Titanic* photographs and that he had been inseparable from his camera in years gone by. Nobody was aware that he had taken nearly 42,000 pictures between 1897 and 1957.

The negatives, all neatly captioned and dated were stored in a trunk in the corner of his room in Milltown. After his death the trunk was deposited in the Jesuit Province Archives in the basement of the

Provincial's house. There it lay unopened for the next twenty-six years.

I had the privilege of unearthing this treasure-trove in 1986. While working at the Provincial's house, I had often seen that trunk lying in the bottom of a press, buried under a few feet of documents. One day, I decided to see what it contained. When I had extricated the trunk, I saw that it bore the legend, in chalked letters: 'Father Browne's Photographs'. Intrigued, I opened the lid. Packs and packs of negatives lay before me. The first one I looked at was captioned 'Pompeii, 1925'. To me, this was like discovering Pompeii itself. I was not surprised some months later when the Features Editor of London's *Sunday Times*, Cal McCrystal, came to view the Collection and dubbed this 'the photographic equivalent to the discovery of the Dead Sea Scrolls.'

Coincidentally, the text of my book *The Annals of Dublin* was with Wolfhound Press, Dublin, awaiting a publication decision at the time. When I informed Seamus Cashman, the publisher, of my discovery which included 4,500 photographs of Dublin taken in the early decades of the century, he came running to investigate. His decision to include Father Browne pictures in *The Annals of Dublin* was instant!

These superb photographs made the book an immediate bestseller. Among the purchasers was one Mary Robinson who bought the volume as a present for her husband, Nicholas. He, in his capacity as Chairman of the Irish Architectural Archive, came to see the architectural photographs contained in the Collection. While staggered by what he saw, Mr Robinson was distressed to see the state of the nitrate negatives. I was shocked to learn that they were deteriorating rapidly, that they would have to be transferred to safety-film without delay.

The very next evening, Mr Robinson brought along his friend David Davison to assess the situation. An expert on the restoration of old photographs, David Davison confirmed that the early negatives were already disintegrating and that the durability of nitrate film was running out fast. He also told me, to my horror, the financial cost of saving the Collection.

It was at this point that the London *Independent* published a full-page feature on Father Browne and his photography. Written by Alan Murdock and Brian Harris (who went on to win the Photographer of the Year award), it stressed the necessity of saving the Collection by putting it on safety-film.

Armed with this material, I approached Allied Irish Bank to seek sponsorship for the salvage operation. I brought out the best in them! AIB-Ireland and AIB-Britain agreed to finance the task jointly. I was instructed to get the work under way immediately. The Jesuits are extremely grateful to Allied Irish Bank for this generous and enlightened sponsorship.

For the next three years, David Davison and his son Edwin, toiled away at saving the negatives and recording the captions on a database system. They managed to save even the oldest negatives before the images disappeared. The Collection is now saved and cross-referenced thanks to their efforts.

In October 1989, the London *Independent* presented a six-page photo-story on Father Browne photographs in its weekend magazine. The reviewer likened the Browne photographs to those of Cartier Bresson, a high compliment indeed. Irish newspapers, national and provincial, were equally forthright in their reviews: as a result, Father Browne photographs appeared on television programmes such as 'Live at 3', the 'Late Late Show' and 'Kenny Live'.

In Autumn 1989, Wolfhound Press published *Father Browne's Ireland* which again received extensive media coverage and again attained bestseller status. It also won the Irish Book Award presented at the National Library, Dublin, that year.

It was early in 1990 that AIB-Britain began to hold exhibitions of Father Browne's photographs, opening in London and moving on to Uxbridge, Nottingham and Manchester. Smaller exhibitions were seen at Frankfurt, Germany and Arles, France, during the course of that year. AIB-Britain also won *The Times* (London) award for the best corporate Christmas card of that year — using a Father Browne skating print.

In 1991, Wolfhound Press published another volume of the Irish photographs, taken in all thirty-two counties, *The Genius of Father Browne*. The *Irish Times* reviewer referred to Father Browne as 'the most important documentary historian of this century'. As a result of this publication, Father Browne photographs appeared not only on RTE television but on British and American channels as well. Photographic essays also appeared in *The Kodak News* and in the prestigious *British Journal of Photography*.

In 1992, Allied Irish Bank used Father Browne photographs for its mass-circulation calendar, as did the Revenue Commissioners in 1994.

Local history societies across Ireland (including those based in Dundalk and Arklow) began to apply for Browne pictures of their area, as did the County Libraries of Leitrim and Galway. The Offaly Historical Society invited me — as the newly-appointed Curator of the Collection — to give an illustrated lecture in Tullamore. Several other specialist bodies (such as the Society of Irish Archivists) followed suit.

Many organisations, commercial and charitable, have used Father Browne photographs to further their work during the past eighteen months. Two in particular would have been particularly gratifying to the photographer: Pavee, the group that looks after the welfare of Ireland's travelling community, has made use of gypsy pictures taken in the early decades of the century; and the Sociology Department of the University of Ulster at Coleraine has used Browne photographs in its 'Ireland Recall' programme of psychogeriatric care. Nurses and occupational therapists have found that these photographs are of definite therapeutic value in encouraging reminiscence.

In the summer of 1992, Ark Life, the assurance subsidiary of Allied Irish Bank, held a series of magnificent exhibitions of Father Browne photographs, opening in Dublin and visiting over twenty towns around Ireland. Ark Life also gave President Mary Robinson a fine framed print, 'Harvest Home' (taken by Father Browne at Molong, New South Wales, in 1924) to bring as a gift on her state visit to Australia later that year.

Before Christmas 1992, the Society of Irish Foresters published *Forest Images: Father Browne's Woodland Photographs* by way of marking its Silver Jubilee.

In February of 1993, the Guinness Group presented a magnificent exhibition of Father Browne's Dublin photographs in its Hop Store exhibition centre at the famous brewery. Called *The Day Before Yesterday*, it displayed over 200 pictures of the capital, taken between the wars, and it attracted large crowds of visitors and excellent reviews. Peter Walsh, Director of the Hop Store, created a most imaginative presentation of the photographs and the exhibition was opened by Mr Nicholas Robinson who described his role in the salvation of the Collection.

The Guinness Group also contributed towards the costs of *Father Browne's Dublin*, published by Wolfhound Press later in 1993. Not exactly the book of the exhibition — although there is a certain amount

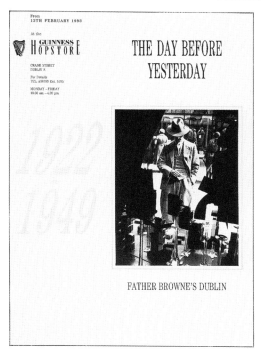
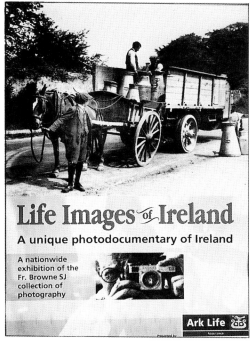

Poster for Guinness Exhibition, 1993, and Ark Life exhibition poster, 1993

of overlap — this volume presents in chronological order a sample of the photographer's Dublin work between 1919 and 1956. Besides reaching bestseller status, *Father Browne's Dublin* received due recognition at the Irish Print Awards ceremony in December 1993.

In Spring 1993, two other exhibition centres put Father Browne photographs on permanent display: Cork Heritage Park has used pictures of horses in its Agricultural Museum and the Cobh Heritage Centre has used enlargements of some of the *Titanic* photographs.

During the Summer of 1993, Ark Life, put on another Father Browne exhibition. Again opening in Dublin, this show toured Ireland like its predecessor the previous year. Twenty venues were selected, and a selection of 'local' photographs was shown wherever the exhibition went. Ark Life donated further sponsorship funds so that a spare set of negatives could be made in case of accident. As Curator of the Collection it is my pleasure to thank Ark Life for ensuring that this important legacy of Father Browne is preserved. Cothú, the Business Council for the Arts, recognised Ark Life's contribution with its Judge's Award for Art Sponsorship, presented by the US ambassador Mrs Jean Kennedy Smith at the Royal Hospital Kilmainham at the end of 1993.

Books
Father's Browne's Ireland, *1989*
Father Browne's Dublin, *1993*
The Genius of Father Browne, *1991*
Forest Images, *1992*
The Annals of Dublin, *1987*

As we go to press, Ark Life has begun to tour Ireland with an enlarged exhibition and RTE has just completed its presentation of six half-hour documentary programmes on the Irish section of the Collection. Directed by Michael O'Connell of ProMedia, the series was also named *The Day before Yesterday* and was launched by the Taoiseach Albert Reynolds. Now the viewing public, naturally, will want to know more about the man behind the camera. My hope is that the present work will fit the bill.

Looking towards the future, we can be certain that many further volumes of Father Browne's photographs will be published in due course. *Father Browne's Australia* and *Father Browne's England* are already in preparation, as is the illustrated story of his voyage on the *Titanic*. I expect that, when the time is ripe, a definitive book will appear, containing the very best of Father Browne's photographs taken world wide. This present work does not set out to do that: rather, the selection here has been made to illustrate the text — but I have no doubt these pictures will impress.